T0291432

"This book looks at what it is like to introduce diversity and inclusion initiatives in a difficult context where oppositional political voices are being shut down. Looking at diversity and inclusion in Turkey is eye-opening and I thoroughly recommend this book to both academics and practitioners of diversity and inclusion around the world. An important book."

Janet Sayers, *Massey University, New Zealand*

Gender Diversity and Inclusion at Work

The purpose of this book is to investigate gender diversity practices and discourse developed by listed companies in Turkey. It pursues this aim by advancing knowledge about business relations affecting workplace gender diversity. The research builds on Bourdieu's field approach and implements a thematic analysis following Braun and Clarke's (2006) guidelines. The findings of the book are based on data collected from unstructured interviews and secondary sources such as the official documents of national and international organisations, newspapers, legislation, and web pages of the related parties. The findings suggest that the implementation of gender diversity practices may require a transformation of perspective and the conditions regarding the political, economic, and cultural realm for realisation of a pervasive movement. Due to the conservative and patriarchal culture, authoritarian rule, and neoliberal policies, gender diversity and inclusion are not seen as issues that should be resolved through the commitment and collaboration of a field. Consequently, diversity management practices are instrumentalised by the business community as a means for corporate communication and image building rather than actively building a diverse workforce.

Zeynep Özsoy built her academic career in Organisation Studies for more than 20 years. She studied business administration at Ankara University and sociology at Middle East Technical University. She is currently the acting dean of Business School at Altınbaş University. The areas she is particularly interested in and has written about include corporate governance practices of Turkish listed companies, boards of directors, diversity management, and alternative organisations.

Mustafa Şenyücel is an assistant professor in Organisation Studies at Haliç University. He studied Computer Engineering, Engineering, and Technology Management and Business Administration at Bahçeşehir, Boğaziçi, and İstanbul Bilgi universities, respectively. He researched organisational field and institutional pluralism at the field that struggles to eliminate violence against women in Turkey. However, he plans to write about the organisational relations between non-governmental organisations, civil society organisations, labour unions, and firms involved in eliminating various other social issues.

Beyza Oba is a professor in Organisation Studies at İstanbul Bilgi University. She studied business administration at Boğaziçi University and İstanbul University. Her main research focus is on the hegemonic struggles of employer unions, trust in interfirm relations, corporate governance practices of Turkish listed companies, and alliance strategies in the open-source software community. She has also written on critical management studies in Turkish business schools.

Routledge Focus on Business and Management

The fields of business and management have grown exponentially as areas of research and education. This growth presents challenges for readers trying to keep up with the latest important insights. *Routledge Focus on Business and Management* presents small books on big topics and how they intersect with the world of business research.

Individually, each title in the series provides coverage of a key academic topic, whilst collectively, the series forms a comprehensive collection across the business disciplines.

Risk Management Maturity
A Multidimensional Model
Sylwia Bąk and Piotr Jedynak

Neuroscience and Entrepreneurship Research
Researching Brain-Driven Entrepreneurship
Víctor Pérez Centeno

Proposal Writing for Business Research Projects
Peter Samuels

Systems Thinking and Sustainable Healthcare Delivery
Ben Fong

Gender Diversity and Inclusion at Work
Divergent Views from Turkey
Zeynep Özsoy, Mustafa Şenyücel and Beyza Oba

For more information about this series, please visit: www.routledge.com/Routledge-Focus-on-Business-and-Management/book-series/FBM

Gender Diversity and Inclusion at Work

Divergent Views from Turkey

Zeynep Özsoy, Mustafa Şenyücel and Beyza Oba

NEW YORK AND LONDON

First published 2023
by Routledge
605 Third Avenue, New York, NY 10158

and by Routledge
4 Park Square, Milton Park, Abingdon, Oxon, OX14 4RN

Routledge is an imprint of the Taylor & Francis Group, an informa business

Library of Congress Cataloging-in-Publication Data
Names: Özsoy, Zeynep, author. | Şenyücel, Mustafa, author. |
Oba, Beyza, author.
Title: Gender diversity and inclusion at work : divergent views from
Turkey / Zeynep Özsoy, Mustafa Şenyücel, and Beyza Oba.
Description: 1 Edition. | New York, NY : Routledge, 2023. | Series:
Routledge focus on business and management | Includes bibliographical
references and index.
Identifiers: LCCN 2022046049 | ISBN 9781032155937 (hardback) |
ISBN 9781032155944 (paperback) | ISBN 9781003244868 (ebook)
Subjects: LCSH: Transgender people—Employment—Turkey. |
Gender nonconformity—Turkey. | Diversity in the workplace—
Turkey. | Discrimination in employment—Turkey.
Classification: LCC HF5549.5.S47 O97 2023 | DDC 331.509561—dc23/
eng/20220922
LC record available at https://lccn.loc.gov/2022046049

ISBN: 978-1-032-15593-7 (hbk)
ISBN: 978-1-032-15594-4 (pbk)
ISBN: 978-1-003-24486-8 (ebk)

DOI: 10.4324/9781003244868

Typeset in Times New Roman
by Apex CoVantage, LLC

Contents

Introduction

They talk diversity and inclusion, but they walk without women

The origins of workforce diversity management can be traced back to the social efforts to eliminate employment discrimination. Management studies questioned the nature of business motivation and argued that the management of cultural diversity, whether voluntary or not, was determined by the quality of Equal Employment Opportunity and Affirmative Action (EEO/AA) law and enforcement mechanisms, ambiguities in legal compliance measures, concerns about litigation, or intentions to fit managerial interests (Edelman, 1992). However, corporate commitment to inclusion and gender diversity is rarely attributed to political, cultural, or socioeconomic conditions or to the meso-level organisational mechanisms of power relations. Recent studies of inclusion and diversity management have been limited to the analysis of the organisational norms and initiatives that identify diversity as a solution for the achievement of organisational effectiveness (for example, Adams & Ferreira, 2009). Even though primary data are from Western democracies, an interest in the study of the corporate practices of Eastern countries has recently emerged (Abdullah et al., 2015; Patrick & Kumar, 2012; Sanan, 2016). This book distinguishes political, cultural, and socioeconomic conditions and organisational relations as the determinants of organisational behaviour for diversity management and inclusion. Consequently, it suggests that the effects of the changes in its political environment with an authoritarian and conservative character, as well as an economy and labour market structure controlled by the intervention of neoliberal ideology, make the Turkish context a unique exemplar for the observation of gender diversity discourse and practices (Buğra & Keyder, 2006; Yılmaz, 2018; Berk & Gumuscu, 2016).

Based on extant studies (for example, Tozkoparan & Vatansever, 2011; Yeşil & Pürtaş, 2017; Sürgevil & Budak, 2008) and our field notes on the prevalent practices of various constituencies such as companies, unions, and non-governmental organisations (NGOs), we claim that in the Turkish context, "diversity" is narrowed down to "gender diversity". Race,

DOI: 10.4324/9781003244868-1

ethnicity, and sexual orientation are still taboo issues (for example, Küskü et al., 2021; Sürgevil & Budak, 2008; Öztürk, 2011). Local and international companies, in line with the political atmosphere and cultural premises, avoid any statements about ethnic minorities and LGBTQIA+ individuals in their publicly announced statements about inclusion practices. These public statements focus on and disclose information only about women. Moreover, companies, academia, NGOs, and unions conceptualise "gender diversity" as "gender equality" or "gender justice" and presume that initiation and practices are state responsibilities, which is framed by related legislation. Thus, in this book, we aim to explore gender diversity and inclusion in Turkey. In so doing, we focus on the practices developed and discourse adopted by the state, publicly listed companies, NGOs, international organisations, and trade unions in promoting a diverse and inclusive work environment. More specifically, the book focuses on the discourses and practices that marginalise women and hinder their employment status by exploring how engaged constituencies attain legitimacy and the power to shape the women's agenda.

In Turkey, the central issue for gender diversity and inclusion is characterised by a competitive business environment inclined to defend extreme opposite regimes. On the one hand, the social democratic environment supports equity in the workplace; on the other, a conservative environment favours male dominance in business and women's traditional roles in society. They defend highly conflicting approaches to women's social and workplace roles, inclusion, and exclusion of the intersectional aspects of women, women's labour force participation, working conditions, as well as collaborative work among stakeholders. The following three quotes, taken from an Islamic-conservative Turkish daily newspaper, a left-wing Turkish daily newspaper, and a left-wing Turkish trade union, respectively, explicate these oppositional opinions, attitudes, and the actions taken.

> The corruption we experience in the family – the core of society –, has never reached such a high level. Trying to force women to work when there is no need has caused great destruction in the family. Acts that would be scandalous in a Muslim state, such as the laws that destroy the family and the Istanbul Convention, are carried out without hesitation.
>
> (Kara, 2019)

> Women are exposed to gender discrimination by being paid less than male employees, being employed in low-status jobs and being assigned lesser duties than men in managerial positions. The victims of physical and sexual violence in the workplace are mostly women. . . . The violence experienced by women in the workplace is often not even a

> subject of complaint due to many reasons such as fear of losing job, not wanting to be the gossip material in the workplace and fear of being exposed to mobbing. However, in this context, the measures to be taken against violence in the workplace and the implementation of the Istanbul Convention will be leading the way.
>
> (Avcı, 2020)

> The political understanding, which does not want to fulfil its obligations, has abolished the contract. . . . It was withdrawn from the Istanbul Convention with a presidential decree at midnight. . . . It is against the Turkish Constitution to repeal a convention that entered into force with the majority of the Grand National Assembly of Turkey (TBMM). . . . . In addition, the Istanbul Convention, the "Right to Life of the Person", regulated in Articles 15 and 17 of the Constitution, is directly related to fundamental rights and freedoms. Therefore, in accordance with Article 104 of the Constitution, issuing a Presidential decree on fundamental rights and freedoms in the Constitution is against the law and has no constitutional basis.
>
> (GENEL-İŞ, 2021)

The issue is especially evident in relation to women, who still encounter numerous discriminatory practices. Our study is built on the presumption that the advancement of women in business life is far too slow in Turkey and much work is to be done to attain a gender diverse and inclusive workplace. For instance, the Global Gender Gap Report (World Economic Forum, 2021) highlights the deepening gender gap in Turkey (133rd out of 156 countries, with a score of 0.638). The report records high rates of unemployment for women, high rates of part-time employment for women (32.8 percent as compared to 18.67 percent for men), low rates of employment for women in top management positions (3.90 percent), and low representation on boards of directors (18.10 percent). In terms of wages, women employees experience a wage gap of 15.6 percent (ILO, 2020) and a "motherhood pay gap" (ILO, 2019). In other words, women's higher education is not translated into higher labour force participation, women are underrepresented in management and leadership roles, women tend to earn less than men for equal work, and women opt out of the workforce to a much higher degree than men. Despite worldwide initiatives to increase gender diversity in the workplace, in Turkey, various actors – state, companies, unions, and NGOs – are reluctant to draft and implement the necessary measures.

Patriarchal norms, neoliberal practices, and the state

The roots of this reluctance can be explained by the traditional values prevalent in Turkish culture that ascribe gender-specific roles, the state policies adopted, and the strategies pursued to reinforce these traditional values and neoliberal policies implemented in the coordination of labour markets. In other words, in Turkey, the patriarchal norms that are diffused throughout the sociopolitical realm and neoliberal policies in the economic realm slow down any progress towards achieving women's inclusion in the workplace. In a patriarchal society like Turkey, the roles traditionally ascribed to women are cleaning, cooking, and taking care of children, husbands, and the elderly, no matter whether those women have a paid job or not. Such an attitude toward the division of work at home "normalises" the unpaid care and domestic labour. The research conducted by Oğuz (2020) on women's paid and unpaid labour in Turkey indicates that qualified women do not search for a job, or they leave the labour market because of their duties at home. Furthermore, the patriarchal norms prevalent at home and within the family surrender women's rights to participate in the labour force to the discretion of the "father" or "husband", and/or women willingly withdraw from the labour market due to internalisation of these norms. At the macro level, patriarchal norms manifest themselves in the policies drafted and discourse utilised by the state authorities in relation to women's employment. In Turkey, the state articulates a discourse that stresses the predominance of family and positions women at home and pursues neoliberal policies with a single-minded purpose, which incentivises companies to employ women in part-time, temporary jobs. In other words, the state has been the major actor in the preservation and endorsement of patriarchy (Tekin, 2020). Especially after 2011, with the drift from "gender equality" to "gender justice" in the official discourse of the state authorities and with the development of institutions (NGOs and state offices) to support traditional gender roles and patriarchal norms, women lost their position in the labour market.

This process was also accentuated by the adoption of the new labour law (4857) in 2003 that legitimised flexible work, part-time work, temporary jobs, and subcontracting. Consequently, women are more and more forced to work in part-time jobs, without job security, and they are usually paid less than male counterparts (Tekin, 2020). Aslan's (2020) study of the İzmir garment industry provides ample evidence that in factories, tasks such as cutting and delivery are taken as men's jobs and men are paid more than women (if there are any women doing these tasks). The lowest paid jobs like packaging are allocated to women workers. In small production units (workshops) in the same industry, cooking and cleaning tasks are done by women employees without payment. Furthermore, employers in the garment industry, in an effort to cut down costs, rely heavily on informal homeworkers comprised of married women with children. The government, in an effort to compensate for the voids that emerged with the weakening of the welfare state, developed social assistance programs such as the Conditional Cash Transfers and General Health Insurance to include informal labour and women in the social security system. However, these devices were adapted by the state cadres to gain support at the elections. Due to the prevalent patriarchal norms, these programs turned out to be instruments for reinforcing women's place, that is, in the home and family. The outcomes of neoliberal policies and their instruments in controlling the labour market (mainly Labour Law 4857) changed the working conditions not only for blue-collar workers but also for white-collar workers comprised of mid-level management cadres and professionals who are drastically influenced as well. White-collar workers became precariats, positioned as workers in the production process working in temporary jobs without job security and with low wages and frequent job changes (Aşçı, 2018; Taşkıran, 2018).

In summary, we claim that the Turkish context provides hindsight into how gender diversity practices can be bent and realigned with the interests of different groups, especially big companies. The Turkish context is characterised by a dominant and authoritarian state and a patriarchal culture that shapes the private and public domain. Perceptions about women and women's place in society are taken for granted and are influential in shaping gender diversity practices. The neoliberal policies implemented after 2011 have left the Turkish economy currently facing a severe crisis whereby most of the listed companies have resorted to austerity measures that limit employment opportunities for women. The implementation of various legislative measures drafted by the current government have meant that women are displaced from workplaces and the public sphere. With various financial incentives (for example, government subsidies for taking care of older family members and grandchildren), women are forced to fulfil domestic care roles and resign from their jobs.

Trade unions; absence of women in management cadres

The analysis of female representation in trade unions has been a challenge for several years, since the state has decided not to utilise a gender filter in general statistics, and union confederations are reluctant to share their gender rates (Kadinişçi, 2021). However, scholarly studies and news reports portray the alarming rates of women's membership in Turkish trade unions

(Ereş & Öztürk, 2020; Urhan, 2017). In a recent interview by Önder (2022) with two women union members, it is stated that:

> For women, who have somehow managed to participate in work life, care responsibilities make it difficult to participate in unions. Surveys show that women have to devote four to five hours a day to housework and care responsibilities, even if they are in a paid job. Home and paid work are actually two separate shifts. Active union work also takes time. Attending union meetings and taking part in union management is like a third shift for women.

Only recently have unions started appointing female presidents. For instance, the Confederation of Revolutionary Trade Unions of Turkey (DISK) has chosen a female president for the first time in its 55-year history. Moreover, according to the news, 2021 was the first time in the history of Turkish unions that a woman also became the head of a union branch (Habertürk, 2021). However, it is also true that the two major workers' confederations, Türk-İş and Hak-İş, still have no female managers at the level of the board of directors, supervisory board, and disciplinary board (Önder, 2022). The agenda of the Turkish trade unions has been burdened with struggles regarding unemployment rates and improvement of working conditions and wages. Union members also acknowledge that corporations are in a competition to fulfil sustainability development goals, so the unions seem to neglect activism on pressuring listed companies towards gender equality practices. However, in a newspaper interview, the president of DISK explains that the recent agenda has been shaped by the annulment of the Istanbul Convention.

> With the Covid-19, the broad definition of female unemployment has reached 43 percent. Almost one in every two women is unemployed. Women's participation in employment declined to 26 percent in Turkey. In other words, only one out of every four women work. The inequalities increase violence against women and femicide more and more. In such processes, while it is necessary to implement policies to eliminate the inequalities and injustices for women . . . the annulment of the Istanbul Convention is unacceptable.
>
> (Evrensel, 2021)

Even so, women members of the unions discuss the male dominance in business as well as the managerial positions of unions that supress women's political advancement. In our opinion, the effects of authoritarian regimes in favour of developing conservative citizenship practices and national identities result in rhetorical constraints, which challenge the democratic character of union relations and impede the regulation of collective agreements towards gender-sensitive business norms.

Non-governmental organisations; advocacy for diversity and inclusion

Especially after 2010, government cadres and the ruling party with an authoritarian approach shifted their discourse and practices from "gender equality" to "gender justice". In the early 2000s, NGOs in Turkey received most of their funding by doing projects funded by international organisations such as the United Nations (UN), the World Bank (WB), and the European Union (EU) that were influential in shaping the agenda towards gender equality in policymaking (Kardam, 2004; Kandiyoti, 2019). For Kandiyoti (2019), the process reflected neoliberal economic and social priorities and resulted in the depoliticisation of feminist demands (Kandiyoti, 2019, p. 88). When the international organisations' agenda started focusing on immigrant and refugee issues, these organisations abandoned Turkish NGO funding. Oppositional NGOs lost power and the Turkish state turned this into an opportunity by supporting the development of "gender justice" discourse and practice with pro-government NGOs that marginalised women's political struggles in relation to gender diversity practices in the business environment. After 2011, the process accelerated and paved the way for temporary work arrangements within private employment offices as well as the regulation of women's roles in society for flexible work with lower wages (Aras, 2013; Mülkiye Haber, 2015). With the inclusion of pro-government, pro-Islamist NGOs in the decision-making process (such as representation at the international organisations), oppositional NGOs were marginalised even more and policy advancements on gender diversity were dragged down. Moreover, organisations representing big capital and a major actor in the implementation of gender diversity practices, such as Turkish Industry and Business Association (TÜSİAD), were also influenced by this process. They also interpreted gender diversity within the framework of justice. A recent report from TÜSİAD (2021) stated that:

> What we aim to achieve [is] . . . A fair Turkey that provides equitable income, eliminates regional disparities, ensures gender equality, where everyone lives equally and freely without discrimination as to language, religion, sect, race, and origin, and does not leave any segment of society behind during the economic development process.

Journalists have interpreted the intentions of these organisations as an instrument for creating competitive advantage over other capital groups

(Oyan, 2021). On the other hand, with the global monitoring towards sustainable development goals, human resource organisations such as Personnel Managers Association (PERYÖN) and consulting firms continue to promote "gender equality" practices via training and giving prizes to companies that support diversity management (PERYÖN, n.d.). However, neither PERYÖN nor consulting firms are as influential as legal regulations in shaping the diversity practices of the listed companies. In short, we can claim that NGOs have been failing to address gender diversity issues over the last ten years.

Listed companies and international organisations

The interest of publicly listed companies in gender diversity was initiated by the Equality at Work Platform which was established in 2012. The big companies that came together for the project, which was supported by the state minister responsible for the family at the time, followed the path drawn up by the platform and mobilised the units responsible for gender diversity in their companies. The issue was taken as the responsibility of human resources and corporate communications. One and a half years after the establishment of the platform, the project was left unassigned when the state minister was appointed to another post and the state cadres' views on gender equality changed. The issue of gender diversity, which is not included in government policies, has become almost entirely a corporate communication issue since 2014.

While big companies compete with one another over their claims of being a woman-friendly company, paradoxically, they are far from fulfilling their legal obligations towards women. The legal rights of female employees to have amenities such as nurseries and breastfeeding rooms are often ignored. In practice, insufficient supervision and low penalties make the laws impotent. Although people who are sensitive to gender diversity in big companies, from time to time, make efforts to carry out various studies for the betterment of women, companies that are profit-oriented by nature do not want to bear the "cost" of such projects. The activities carried out through the human resources departments of most of the companies are limited to communication activities and training to empower women and raise awareness among men. Efforts have been very limited, especially in companies operating in fields that traditionally employ men and exclude women. Such companies preferred to carry out social responsibility projects for women rather than taking necessary steps towards gender equality within the company. These projects are largely related to developing the capacities and skills of, especially, young women.

International organisations, especially the UN, play a leading role in diversity management in Turkey, as well as in the rest of the world. These organisations develop and run joint projects with companies and many other local stakeholders. However, unless these efforts are supported by the state and, more importantly, unless legal regulations are enacted, the activities of international organisations on gender diversity cannot go beyond public-opinion-forming activities.

Why and how to study gender diversity in Turkey

Given this background, we think that the diversity management field in Turkey provides a valuable example about how diversity management practices narrowed down to "gender diversity" and diversity management practices are limited to compliance with the related legislation. The Turkish case for gender diversity also differs from examples in other geographic areas – not only because it is immersed in a neoliberal, authoritarian context, but also because of the prevalence of patriarchal norms. The field is shaped by and evolves with neoliberal practices in controlling the labour market, their authoritarian implementation by the state cadres, and deep-rooted patriarchal norms underlining the attitudes towards women and women's place in society.

Currently, there are a limited number of publications on diversity management in Turkey. Turkish publications are generally academic journal articles, and they tend to ignore the complexity of the political, cultural, and legal environment that shapes diversity practices. In contrast, in this book, we focus on gender diversity from a much broader perspective, across different sectors and hierarchical positions, and investigate the various practices developed to promote a diverse workforce. Furthermore, by focusing on the actions and discourses of different constituencies engaged in diversity management, we provide a more comprehensive understanding of the power relationships shaping women's employment and their inclusion in the workplace.

Borrowing on the tradition of Bourdieu's (2005) field approach, in this book we take diversity management as a field, where various constituencies position themselves in terms of their discourse and actions. Such an approach is useful in identifying practices that reinforce the gender gap and the neglect of gender diversity practices. In all the chapters, rather than listing what has been done, the focus is on why such actions have been taken. What are the drivers behind these actions? How are responses shaped? How are they aligned with the demands of other constituencies? All arguments are consolidated with statements from interviewees, vignettes, and secondary sources to further explain the effects of an authoritative and neoliberal order, male-dominated cultural and conservative norms within the national realm, as well as the consequences of relationships with international organisations.

We started our longitudinal research by studying publicly listed companies, their discourse and practices related to diversity management. As we proceeded with our interviews and analysis of public announcements (such as web pages and the public speeches of the top managers), we decided to extend our survey to include state trade unions, NGOs, and international organisations since the actions taken and discourse developed by listed companies are heavily influenced by the positions taken and policies drafted by these constituencies. We conducted unstructured interviews with the top managers, human resources directors of publicly listed companies, managers of unions and specialists working in unions, consultants, and representatives of international organisations who occupy a position that exclusively deals with gender diversity initiatives. Approaching these different interviewees has been useful in representing both differing and similar opinions around diversity management and gender diversity issues raised by our research. As secondary sources – besides web pages of listed companies, NGOs, official labour statistics, reports of international organisations concerned with women's employment status (such as the Organisation for Economic Co-operation and Development [OECD] and the International Labour Organisation [ILO]), newspaper articles, and legal documents – we followed platforms initiated and maintained by oppositional groups such as the Women's Platform for Equality (EŞİK) and the Women's Platform for Equality and Justice (SES) and platforms of alternative media such as 1+1. EŞİK, SES, and 1+1 Express were especially useful in documenting cases, providing evidence for workplace gender issues such as the dire working conditions, discriminatory practices, and the work life experienced by women employees.

References

Abdullah, S. N., Ku Ismail, K. N. I., & Nachum, L. (2015). Does having women on boards create value? The impact of societal perceptions and corporate governance in emerging markets. *Strategic Management Journal*, 37(3), 466–476. https://doi.org/10.1002/smj.2352

Adams, R. A., & Ferreira, D. (2009). Women in the boardroom and their impact on governance and performance. *Journal of Financial Economics*, 94(2), 291–309. https://doi.org/10.1016/j.jfineco.2008.10.007

Aras, Z. (2013). *AKP'nin "Kadın İstihdam Paketi"* [AKP's "Women Employment Package"]. Retrieved from https://marksist.net/zehra-aras/akpnin-kadin-istihdam-paketi.htm

Aşçı, M. S. (2018). Precarious work, precariat and excluded personnel. *Journal of Industrial Policy and Technology Management*, 1(2), 99–114.

Aslan, A. (2020). Kapitalist ataerkilin ablukasında kadınların sınıf deneyimleri: İzmir konfeksiyon sektöründe üretim süreçlerinin ve gündelik hayatın cinsiyetçi yapısı [Women's class experiences under the siege of capitalist patriarchy: The general nature of production processes and everyday life in İzmir's garment sector]. *Praxis*, 52(1), 135–156.

Avcı, D. (2020). İşyerinde şiddet, ayrımcılık ve İstanbul sözleşmesi [Violence in the workplace, discrimination and the Istanbul Convention]. *Ekmek ve Gül*. Retrieved from https://ekmekvegul.net/dergi/isyerinde-siddet-ayrimcilik-ve-istanbul-sozlesmesi

Berk, E., & Gumuscu, S. (2016). Rising competitive authoritarianism in Turkey. *Third World Quarterly*, 37(9), 1581–1606. https://doi.org/10.1080/01436597.2015.1135732

Bourdieu, P. (2005). *The Social Structures of the Economy*. Polity Press.

Buğra, A., & Keyder, Ç. (2006). The Turkish welfare regime in transformation. *Journal of European Social Policy*, 16(3), 211–228. https://doi.org/10.1177/0958928706065593

Edelman, L. B. (1992). Legal ambiguity and symbolic structures: Organizational mediation of civil rights law. *American Journal of Sociology*, 97(6), 1531–1576. Retrieved from www.jstor.org/stable/2781548

Ereş, G., & Öztürk, M. (2020). Kadınların sendikalarda görev almada karşılaştıkları sorunlara yönelik bir çalışma [A study on the problems faced by women in employment in trade unions]. *Süleyman Demirel Üniversitesi İktisadi ve İdari Bilimler Fakültesi Dergisi*, 25(1), 71–88. Retrieved from https://dergipark.org.tr/tr/pub/sduiibfd/issue/53017/705161

Evrensel. (2021). *DİSK Başkanı Arzu Çerkezoğlu: Haklarımız için mücadeleye devam edeceğiz!* [DİSK President Arzu Çerkezoğlu: We Will Continue to Fight for Our Rights!]. Retrieved from www.evrensel.net/haber/428709/disk-baskani-arzu-cerkezoglu-haklarimiz-icin-mucadeleye-devam-edecegiz

GENEL-İŞ. (2021). *İstanbul sözleşmesinin yürürlükten kaldırılması hukuksuzdur* [The Annulment of the Istanbul Convention is Unlawful!]. Retrieved from www.genel-is.org.tr/istanbul-sozlesmesinin-yururlukten-kaldirilmasi-hukuksuzdur,2,46007#.YteqlXZByUk

Habertürk. (2021). *İlk kez bir kadın sendika şube başkanı oldu* [For the First Time, a Woman Became the Head of a Union Branch]. Retrieved from www.haberturk.com/kadin-sendikacinin-basarisi-3039522-ekonomi

ILO. (2019). *A Quantum Leap for Gender Equality: For a Better Future of Work for All*. International Labour Office.

ILO. (2020). *Measuring the Gender Wage Gap: Case of Turkey, ILO Turkey Office and TurkStat*. Retrieved from www.ilo.org/ankara/publications/WCMS_756660/lang-en/index.htm

Kadınişçi. (2021). *Sendika İstatistikleri yayımlandı: Kadınlar nerede* [Union Statistics Released: Where Are the Women]. Retrieved from www.kadinisci.org/orgutlenme-sendika/sendika-istatistikleri-yayimlandi-kadinlar-nerede/

Kandiyoti, D. (2019). Against all odds: The resilience and fragility of women's gender activism in Turkey, in Kandiyoti, D., Al-Ali, N. and Poots, K. S. (eds.), *Gender, Governance and Islam*, Edinburgh University Press, 80–100. https://doi.org/10.1515/9781474455459

Kara, V. (2019). İstanbul sözleşmesi ve aileyi yok etmek için alınan kararlar [Istanbul convention and decisions taken to destroy the family]. *Akit*. Retrieved from www.yeniakit.com.tr/yazarlar/vehbi-kara/istanbul-sozlesmesi-ve-aileyi-yok-etmek-icin-alinan-kararlar-29588.html

Kardam, N. (2004). The emerging global gender equality regime from neoliberal and constructivist perspectives in international relations. *International Feminist Journal of Politics*, 6(1), 85–109. http://doi.org/10.1080/1461674032000165941

Küskü, F., Aracı, Ö., & Özbilgin, M. F. (2021). What happens to diversity at work in the context of a toxic triangle? Accounting for the gap between discourses and practices of diversity management. *Human Resource Management Journal*, 31(2), 553–574. https://doi.org/10.1111/1748-8583.12324

Mülkiye Haber. (2015). *Özel istihdam büroları kadınlar için çözüm mü?* [Are Private Employment Agencies the Solution for Women?]. Retrieved from https://mulkiyehaber.net/ozel-istihdam-burolari-kadinlar-icin-cozum-mu/

Oğuz, S. (2020). İşgücü anketlerinden Türkiye'de ücretli-ücretsiz kadın emeği üzerine gözlemler: 2008 krizinin etkileri [Observations on women's paid and unpaid labour in Turkey from labour force surveys: Effects of 2008 crises]. *Praxis*, 52(1), 35–68.

Önder, A. (2022). Toplumsal cinsiyet eşitsizliklerini görmezden gelen sendikalar güç kaybediyor [Unions that ignore gender inequalities are losing power]. *Kadınişçi*. Retrieved from www.kadinisci.org/orgutlenme-sendika/toplumsal-cinsiyet-esitsizliklerini-gormezden-gelen-sendikalar-guc-kaybediyor/

Öztürk, M. (2011). Sexual orientation discrimination: Exploring the experiences of lesbian, gay and bisexual employees in Turkey. *Human Relations, 64*(8), 1099–1118. https://doi.org/10.1177/0018726710396249

Oyan, O. (2021). *Patronların raporu: Türkiye'nin değil 'TUSİAD'ın geleceğinin inşası'* [The Bosses' Report: 'Building the Future of TUSAAD, Not Turkey']. Retrieved April 4, 2022, from https://haber.sol.org.tr/haber/gorus-patronlarin-raporu-turkiyenin-degil-TUSİADin-geleceginin-insasi-316509.

Patrick, H. A., & Kumar, V. R. (2012). *Managing Workplace Diversity: Issues and Challenges*. SAGE Open.

PERYÖN. (n.d.). *Peryön İnsana Değer Ödülleri* [Peryön Human Value Awards Award Categories]. Retrieved from www.peryon.org.tr/odul-kategorileri

Sanan, N. K. (2016). Board gender diversity. Financial and social performance of Indian firms. *Vision*, 20(4), 361–367.

Sürgevil, O., & Budak, G. (2008). İşletmelerin farklılıkların yönetimi anlayışına yaklaşım tarzlarının saptanmasına yönelik bir araştırma [A research on determining approaches to management of diversity in businesses]. *Dokuz Eylül Üniversitesi Sosyal Bilimler Enstitüsü Dergisi*, 10(4), 65–96. Retrieved from https://arastirmax.com/en/system/files/dergiler/591/makaleler/10/4/arastirmax-isletmelerin-farkliliklarin-yonetimi-anlayisina-yaklasim-tarzlarinin-saptanmasina-yonelik-bir-arastirma.pdf

Taşkiran, G. (2018). Alternative labor organisations with precarious. *International Journal of Current Research*, 10(11), 75093–75101. https://doi.org/10.24941/ijcr.32841.11.2018

Tekin, C. (2020). Atölyeden eve: Fason üretimin iki ucundaki kadınların sömürü-güçlenme ikilemi [From workshop to home: The dilemma of subcontracting women workers between empowerment and exploitation]. *Praxis*, 52(1), 115–134.

Tozkoparan, G., & Vatansever, Ç. (2011). Farklılıkların yönetimi: İnsan kaynakları yöneticilerinin farklılık algısı üzerine bir odak grup çalışması [Diversity management: A focus group study of perception of diversity among human resource managers]. *Akdeniz Üniversitesi İktisadi ve İdari Bilimler Fakültesi Dergisi*, 21, 89–109. Retrieved from https://dergipark.org.tr/en/pub/auiibfd/issue/32324/359211

TÜSİAD. (2021). *Building the Future with a New Mindset: People, Science, Institutions*. Retrieved May 5, 2022, from https://TUSİAD.org/en/reports/item/10864-building-the-future-with-a-new-mindset-executive-summary

Urhan, B. (2017). Sendika içi demokrasi ve sendika içi kadın örgütlenmesi [Intra-union democracy and intra-union women's organization]. *Journal of Social Policy Conferences*, 29–58. Retrieved from https://dergipark.org.tr/en/pub/iusskd/issue/33251/370114

World Economic Forum. (2021). *Global Gender Gap Report 2021*. Retrieved from www.weforum.org/reports/global-gender-gap-report-2021

Yeşil, S., & Pürtaş, S. (2017). Farklılıkların yönetimi, kurumsal itibar ve işletme performansı üzerine etkileri: Tekstil sektöründe bir alan araştırması [The effects of diversity management on corporate reputation and firm performance: A field study in textile industry]. *Kahramanmaraş Sütçü İmam Üniversitesi İktisadi ve İdari Bilimler Fakültesi Dergisi*, 7(2), 173–194. Retrieved from http://iibfdergisi.ksu.edu.tr/en/pub/issue/33603/372960

Yılmaz, Z. (2018). The AKP and the new politics of the social: Fragile citizenship, authoritarian populism and paternalist family policies. In *Populism and the Crisis of Democracy* (pp. 150–167). Routledge.

1 Global and local perspectives on gender diversity

Introduction

Global progress towards closing the gender gap in the workplace is slow. According to the estimates of the World Economic Forum (WEF) (2021), if wage equality and labour markets are managed at today's pace, more than 250 years of work will be needed to eliminate employment inequality. Scholarly research and supraorganisational work also support this prediction with discussions about the lack of gender diversity in specific fields including science, technology, engineering, mathematics, and medicine (STEMM) (Chaudhry et al., 2019; Holman et al., 2018) and transportation (European Commision et al., 2019). When Noland et al. (2016) questioned whether it is profitable for companies to assign women to executive positions, eight-year-old Reuters data representing 91 countries revealed that more than half of the participant firms had no female board and C-suite members. The most recent Gender Diversity Index (EWOB, 2021) shows that there has not been much change since then. It is evident in the report that, in Europe, the share of women occupying executive positions is far behind the aims of the European Union Gender Equality Strategy for 2025 (European Commission, 2020). Although global studies have revealed how women in the workforce can positively impact an economy by sparking continued growth and productivity, companies are sceptical about creating gender equality at executive and board levels (for example, Chandrasekar, 2021; Döğer, 2022; Gender Diversity Index, 2021; Toossi & Morisi, 2017). Sources have highlighted the long-term outcomes of skill shortages and poverty as competitive disadvantages in the post-pandemic period that can be avoided with the inclusion of more women in the labour market (CED, 2022; European Commission, 2020; Hyrynsalmi & Sutinen, 2019; Jackson, 2022; Ngwakwe, 2020). This finding also suggests that the performance of national/regional economies will be improved, and individual social rights will be secured.

DOI: 10.4324/9781003244868-2

Working conditions are no less alarming than women's employment opportunities. Leaving aside outdated ideas that assume women favour jobs with low skills needs over demanding career options (Grönlund & Öun, 2018), a work-life literature review of Perry-Jenkins and Gerstel (2020) shows that current working conditions such as longer working hours and alternative work arrangements such as remote work deepen gender inequality. Role expectations have not changed in dramatic ways, and women are still expected to take childcare and elder-care responsibilities. Therefore, women expend more effort managing work-life balance conflicts (Young & Scheiman, 2018). Indeed, the early Covid-19 period increased the pressures on women to prioritise childcare with the closure of nurseries and schools. Accordingly, empirical studies demonstrated that the working hours of women significantly dropped and resulted in further gender gaps (Collins et al., 2020; Hanzl & Rehm, 2021; Yildirim & Eslen-Ziya, 2021). For example, Bonacini et al. (2021) argued that the pandemic environment caused an increase in teleworking settings and income inequalities, which older male workers mostly benefited from. Thus, in post-pandemic resilience times, firms will form hybrid work structures (such as onsite/remote work models, double shifts, flextime, compressed workweeks; see SHRM, 2022; WEF, 2021), which will pose conflicts for women in managing work and household responsibilities.

Global perspectives

As a reflection of the global deterioration in the economic realm and the transformations in business practices, gender diversity scholars continue to seek clarification of the relationship between gender-balanced workforces and corporate economic performance. This relationship has started to attract scholarly attention within management and organisation studies in the last 30 years. Earlier focus was on the cultural diversity of teams regarding interactions (for example, Larkey, 1996), power and status (Ely & Thomas, 2001), goals and outcomes like organisational attachment (for example, Tsui et al., 1992), or productivity (for example, Chatman et al., 1998). With the advancement of these studies, academic attention to board gender composition increased. Yet, management research could not report direct causality between work group and team gender composition and corporate performance. Instead, researchers emphasised mediated effects such as business strategies, organisational culture, and human resource practices, which are specific to the macro context examined (for example, see Kochan et al., 2003). In this vein, Norwegian and Spanish contexts have received the most attention due to the gender quota regulations prevalent in these countries. For instance, Campbell and Minguez-Vera (2008) found positive effects of board diversity in Spanish business sectors and stated that a gender balance at the board level has the most beneficial effect for improving company value. In comparison, studies of the US context revealed negative effects of quotas. Even though a female presence in monitoring functions was found effective, Adam and Ferreira (2009) reported that company performance decreased when board gender diversity increased. The study revealed the negative effects of excessive monitoring and gender quota practice at well-governed firms. However, more recent board gender diversity studies also revealed positive outcomes. Recent studies demonstrate that companies could see positive outcomes when they have 30 percent or more women members on the board (Joecks et al., 2013; Wiley & Monllor-Tormos, 2018). In short, studies focused on board gender composition reveal that a female presence in the boardroom positively affects profitability or return on assets (ROA) and growth (for example, see Terjesen et al., 2016; Conyon & He, 2017).

This is a global concern for trade unions, where leaders could not integrate policies and practices fully into diversity-oriented systems (for more details, see Kirton & Greene, 2022, Greene, & Kirton, 2004; Ibsen & Tapia, 2017). Although stakeholders like governmental agencies, NGOs, trade unions, and international organisations take pivotal roles in fostering equal opportunities, they are also the most neglected players in gender diversity literature. More observations are needed in order to have a deeper understanding of the roles and influences of various constituencies for a more diverse workplace. As claimed by Tatli (2011), these observations should be guided by interorganisational as well as intersectional perspectives since there are only a few guidelines for stakeholders to address how gender diversity practices within corporations can be translated to economic and social outcomes beneficial for all stakeholders.

Lastly, diversity is mostly interpreted as women's presence in the labour market and executive functions, which in our opinion is not an inclusive interpretation. It is fruitful to examine ethnicity and race, sexual orientation, and other surface-level diversity variables to incorporate an intersectional understanding. With increasing immigration, changing demographic patterns, and the proliferation of skilled ethnic groups, firms have become more interested in recruiting a racially and culturally diverse workforce (Oerlemans et al., 2008). However, research also suggests that discrimination against ethnic/racial minority groups concerning issues like inequal hiring, promotion and pay, harassment, and other sources of oppression persist in various sectors (Nunez-Smith et al., 2009; Osseo-Asare et al., 2018) and in various countries. For example, a Di Stasio and Larsen (2020) study shows how women of colour were significantly disadvantaged in the hiring processes even for occupations mostly associated with women. Furthermore, interest in comprehending sexual diversity is increasing among academicians working on organisations and management (Byington et al., 2021). For instance, Palmer et al.

(2021) debated the pervasiveness of stereotypes in academic fields related to science, technology, engineering, and mathematics (STEM), where most participants associated technical skills and roles with heterosexual men. These assumptions may prevent people with a sexually diverse orientation from challenging not only STEM sectors, but also other business environments where similar stereotypes exist. Scholarly discussions about discriminatory barriers and employment outcomes for transgender and other gender-diverse people suggest that not only the roles attributed to work, but also limitations of governmental policies and discriminatory business practices continue to affect these women (for example, see, Isaacs et al., 2020; Nelson et al., 2021).

Local perspectives

According to the Global Gender Gap Index 2021 prepared by the WEF, there is a deepening gap in the inclusion of women in the labour force as professionals, technical workers, legislators, and senior and top managers. Furthermore, as indicated by the same report, in the workplace, women are paid less than men for similar work, more women are employed in part-time jobs, and dire working conditions (for example, short duration for maternity leave and absence of nursery services at the workplaces) restrict women's participation in the labour market. Given this background, academic work on the gender diversity practices of Turkish companies can be grouped into two streams: Diversity in the workplace and diversity in the boardroom.

Diversity in the workplace

Throughout the last two decades, Turkish management scholars have been interested in studying gender diversity in business. However, they attempted to generalise their findings without considering context-specific factors; they only recorded their observations regarding gender diversity practices taking place within the companies. The extant literature lacks historical specificity of inclusion and gender diversity practices in Turkey. Instead, these studies mainly borrow the assumptions of studies conducted in other geographic areas. For instance, Yeşil and Pürtaş (2017) argue that the industrialisation of the workforce is the primary factor, and Özbilgin (2015) identifies the global diffusion of neoliberal policies and resource needs as the main dynamic that directed Turkish business attention towards diversity management. The common theme in these studies is globalisation (for example, see İnce et al., 2015; Sürgevil & Budak, 2008; Tozkoparan & Vatansever, 2011; Usta & Bayraktar, 2017). Accordingly, it is assumed that globalisation has pressured local organisations into learning how to work in multicultural environments (Özkaya et al., 2008) and develop assets supporting inclusive practices (Kevser, 2019).

Another group of studies on gender diversity focuses on the antecedents of diversity practices adopted by Turkish companies. Borrowing on the context-specific issues identified in other geographic areas, these studies try to explain why Turkish companies opt for diversity management. In other words, these studies, rather than identifying Turkish context-specific factors as the promoters of workplace diversity practices, look for the presence/absence of variables studied in other contexts. These studies focus on changes in population (Özkaya et al., 2008), workforce composition (İnce et al., 2015; Sürgevil & Budak, 2008; Tozkoparan & Vatansever, 2011), emerging interests of local organisations working on equal rights and opportunities (Özkaya et al., 2008), the diffusion of multinational companies (Tozkoparan & Vatansever, 2011), international mergers and acquisitions (Kılıç, 2015), and international business operations (Kevser, 2019) as the major antecedents of diversity management practices in the Turkish workplace. In a similar vein, the Sürgevil and Budak (2008) study underlines the role of increasing anti-discrimination practices, emphasis on equal opportunities, and positive action in the US context, while Tozkoparan and Vatansever (2011) focus on the recognition and implementation of the same issues in Canada, Australia, and the EU as the drivers of diversity management in Turkey. The abundance of conceptualisations adopted by the Turkish scholars that lack the influences of meso-level contextual factors complicates understanding about the diffusion of diversity management in the Turkish business context.

Other empirical research studies explore the causality between diversity management and some performance indicators. The findings of these studies illustrate that successful implementation of diversity can lead to a competitive advantage (Özkaya et al., 2008). They also demonstrate that if diversity practices are effectively reflected to customers, they can have positive outcomes (Özkaya et al., 2008). Similarly, Yeşil and Pürtaş (2017) in their study of a textile company explicate how strategies for developing employee assets can lead to successful reputation management. According to this study, besides creating a competitive advantage, a good reputation, and a reliable customer base, the presence of more women in the upper echelons improves company value, secures the needs and rights of the minority shareholders (Yağlı & Ünlü, 2019), and attracts new "talent" to the company (Ince et al., 2015).

Existing studies interpret the initiation of diversity management in Turkey as initiated by multinational companies (MNC). For example, in Tozkoparan and Vatansever's (2011) study, HR managers of MNCs operating in Istanbul explained that they were involved in various practices, such as the removal of operations that could be interpreted as discriminatory and the development of equal evaluation procedures for personnel performance, as well as awareness-raising, communication, and empathy training. The study also revealed that company gender practices included parenting seminars and the establishment of nursery rooms. Recruitment of local HR experts who are familiar with the local laws, culture, and political and economic environment of Turkey or the adaptation of foreign diversity policies are cited as the main diversity practices exercised by the subsidiaries (Yağlı & Ünlü, 2019).

Based on extant research and our field notes, we have seen that in the Turkish context, gender is usually evaluated alongside other diversity dimensions like age, disability, victims of terror, ex-convicts, education status, marital status, or seniority. The reason for such a stance is rooted in the Turkish legal system, and companies are inclined to demonstrate their compliance with laws. Turkish companies mainly assume a law-abiding stance while aiming to maximise shareholder value. In so doing, other stakeholder concerns, especially the concerns of the employees which can lead to an increase in costs, are neglected. As reported by some studies (for example, Sürgevil & Budak, 2008), HR managers are reluctant to implement gender diversity practices other than those specified by legislation since there are no pressures from rivals or government authorities. As indicated by Özsoy et al., (2019), companies still favour fulfilling the requirements of the law and are not inclined to advance their gender diversity practices beyond that.

Also, the diversity and inclusion rhetoric of some Turkish holding companies presents diversity management as an international business norm, which demonstrates commitment to sustainability and corporate social responsibility goals (for instance, see the annual report and investor relations report of Akbank, n.d.a). These norms emphasise valuing employees (Koç Holding, n.d.), commitment to social gender equality (Akbank, n.d.b.; Arçelik, 2021), creating a corporate culture for strengthening the position of women (Akbank, n.d.b.; Arçelik, 2021), and a commitment to anti-discriminatory recruiting procedures. Companies also recognised the positive outcomes of diversity management, like developing a productive and collaborative workforce, opportunities to drive sustainable improvements, developing creative thinking, and aligning with the interests of stakeholders (Koç Holding, n.d.). Turkish holding companies emphasised positive discrimination by providing benefits for women in terms of mentoring programs on maternity, nursery services, workplace safety improvements, training on gender norms (Koç Holding, n.d.), encouraging the full use of maternity leave, and ensuring a return to work with the same position and conditions (Akbank, n.d.b). Given these public disclosures of some holding companies, the abovementioned law-abiding attitude adopted, and the practices of MNCs, we can say that the Turkish diversity management landscape is marked with divergence in discourse and practice. Lastly, we also see that intersectional understanding is absent in Turkish diversity management practices. This is likely because companies rarely consider and take action towards the rights of minorities in the workplace. Previous studies support this, as scholars mention that only a few managerial respondents considered surface-level diversity variables such as race, ethnicity, or sexual orientation as part of their firm diversity practices (for example, see Özsoy et al., 2019; Küskü et al., 2021). However, it is detrimental for companies to neglect intersectionality. For instance, since the legal, regulatory, and social environment fails to address sexual minority rights, it is argued that sexual orientation discrimination has been diffused throughout the Turkish work environment (Öztürk, 2011). Discriminatory perceptions towards LGBTQ-I members are still observed (Küçükaltan et al., 2020), and discriminatory acts are exercised in various organisational practices from recruitment to promotions (Özgünlü, 2019).

Diversity in the boardroom

The global emphasis on gender diversity in the boardroom and company performance also found its way into academic circles in Turkey. The majority of the research conducted in this vein focused on the outcomes of gender diversity in the boardroom on the financial performance of the firms. Quantitative data provided by these studies led the readers to consider that gender diversity is a mixed blessing. Some empirical evidence in the banking industry reported that gender diversity had positively influenced the banks' financial performance, such as ROA or return on equity (ROE). However, these studies tended to avoid political and economic discussions originating from the particularities of the Turkish context (for example, Otluoğlu et al., 2016; Yağlı & Ünlü 2019). Others who used similar variables also found negative outcomes, and in a similar way, ruled out the Turkish social and political context (for example, Kılıç, 2015). Only a few of these studies suggested a neutral impact of gender diversity on financial outcomes, either on accounting-based performance in general (for example, Karayel & Doğan, 2014) or on firm value specifically (Yağlı & Ünlü, 2019). Similarly, as is the case with diversity management, the findings are based on the assumptions derived from international research and not the critical evaluation of the sociopolitical and/or political economy conditions faced by Turkish firms.

Apart from accounting performances, several other research studies mentioned sustainability regulations as an inducement to gender representation in the boardroom (for example, Otluoğlu et al., 2016; Yıldız et al., 2019). The Corporate Governance Directive of (Turkish) Capital Markets Board article 4.3.9 recommends that publicly listed companies increase the number of women on the board to at least 25 percent (SPK, 2014). However, none of the interviewees or informants for this study referred to this regulation. Furthermore, the corporate governance monitoring report of the Capital Markets Board (CMB, 2020) reported that compliance rates of the monitored

BIST 100 and 30 companies did not even reach 15 percent. This may be seen as evidence of the fact that recommendations stay on paper and the pressure in the business environment to advance gender diversity is not influential.

Intersectional perspectives are almost completely absent in the extant Turkish literature on board studies. While the presence of foreign directors in the boardroom received attention, the race, ethnicity, and sexual orientation of board members are still taboo issues. For example, the Colakoglu et al. (2020) study revealed that the poor performance on corporate social responsibility was due to the absence of foreign members on Turkish boards. Moreover, Karayel and Doğan (2016) debated the argument that the increase in foreign members would have a significant positive effect on ROA and ROE. However, the Kılıç (2015) study reported negative effects of foreign member presence on financial performance in the banking industry. According to Kılıç (2015), the reasons for this negative relationship could be explained as the lack of knowledge and involvement in local issues by the foreign board members. Thus, it could be claimed that a typical Turkish boardroom intersectionality is reduced to the presence of foreign members. On the contrary, in practice, according to the public announcements of some of the biggest Turkish companies, we can say that they visualise gender diversity as an important part of their board composition. These companies claim that for sustainable growth, developments in brand culture, and the improvement of the decision-making processes, there should be equality in wages and board composition. Boards are anticipated to be represented by women with diverse knowledge, skills, industry experience, and professional background. Moreover, Turkish holding companies which promoted women's representation in board composition revealed several commitments. For instance, according to Mavi (2021), an international textile company with headquarters in Turkey committed to appointing women to hold onethird of the seats on its board of directors by 2024. According to a study by Arçelik (2021, May 25), a household appliances producer aimed to increase its number of female executives to 25 percent by 2026. Although these issues are discussed in the following chapters, at this stage, we can say that diversity management in the boardroom in Turkey is reduced to gender equality in numbers. In a way, women's presence in the boardroom is adopted by Turkish companies for reputation building and branding.

Conclusion

Not only is the decreasing participation of females in the workforce a concern for Turkey, but it also is a major concern for economic, sustainable growth worldwide. Global economic crises and the pandemic era resulted in poverty and skill shortages that could be overcome with women in the workforce.

Interestingly, companies are competitive in terms of fulfilling the 17 goals of sustainable development, but they are hesitant to employ women in many sectors and to promote women to managerial positions. This is a contradictory aspect if we consider that gender equality and women's empowerment are the common requirements to fulfil every sustainable development goal. Furthermore, as we also mentioned above, the academic literature on gender board diversity and diversity management revealed mixed results regarding the impact of women on the economic performance of firms, which does not help women's emancipation in work-life at all. In such turmoil, many women still face a gender gap in employment, income, and promotion opportunities, as well as worsening working conditions, discrimination, exclusion, and violence, while many of them struggle to balance work-life responsibilities and manage childcare and elder care. Thus, this work is vital for understanding how an organisational field responds to gender diversity when it has stakeholders from the government and its agencies to non-governmental and international organisations, trade unions, and listed companies. Only a few studies considered multiple layers of the business environments in understanding diversity (Tatli, 2011; Kirton & Greene, 2022), and more work has to be done to fully explain inclusion in the workplace. In the following chapters, you will learn more about the Turkish context and how its organisations have responded to gender diversity and inclusion in the workplace, as a means to help you consider future solutions.

References

Adams, R. B., & Ferreira, D. (2009). Women in the boardroom and their impact on governance and performance. *Journal of financial economics*, 94(2), 291–309. https://doi.org/10.2139/ssrn.1107721

Akbank. (n.d.a). *Akbank Integrated Annual Report*. Akbank J.C.S. Retrieved March 14, 2022, from www.akbankinvestorrelations.com/en/sustainability/year-list/Sustainability-reports/60/0/0

Akbank. (n.d.b). *Our Understanding of Diversity and Inclusion*. Akbank J.C.S. Retrieved March 14, 2022, from www.akbankinvestorrelations.com/en/images/pdf/Akbank_Diversity_and_inclusion.pdf

Arçelik. (2021, May 25). *Arçelik yönetim kurulu çeşitlilik politikası* [Arçelik's Board of Directors Diversity Policy]. Arçelik J.C.S. Retrieved March 14, 2022, from www.arcelikglobal.com/media/6313/arcelik-yk-cesitlilik-politikasi_25521_.pdf

Bonacini, L., Gallo, G., & Scicchitano, S. (2021). Working from home and income inequality: Risks of a "new normal" with COVID-19. *Journal of Population Economics*, 34, 303–360. https://doi.org/10.1007/s00148-020-00800-7

Byington, E. K., Tamm, G. F., & Trau, R. N. (2021). Mapping sexual orientation research in management: A review and research agenda. *Human Resource Management*, 60(1), 31–53. https://doi.org/10.1002/hrm.22026

Campbell, K., & Minguez-Vera, A. (2008). Gender diversity in the boardroom and firm financial performance. *Journal of Business Ethics*, 83, 435–451. https://doi.org/10.1007/s10551-007-9630-y

Chatman, J. A., Polzer, J. T., Barsade, S. G., & Neale, M. A. (1998). Being different yet feeling similar: The influence of demographic composition and organizational culture on work processes and outcomes. *Administrative Science Quarterly*, 43(4), 749–780. https://doi.org/10.2307/2393615

CED. (2022). *CED Policy Watch: The US Labor Shortage – Tackling the Challenge*. Committee for Economic Development of The Conference Board. Retrieved May 10, 2022, from www.ced.org/solutions-briefs/the-us-labor-shortage-a-plan-to-tackle-the-challenge

Chandrasekar, S. (2021). Women and work. *Indian Journal of Occupational and Environmental Medicine*, 25(1), 1–3. Retrieved from www.ijoem.com/text.asp?2021/25/1/1/314649

Chaudhry, H., Wall, A. E., & Wall, J. L. (2019, July). Exploring the gender gap in tech companies: Why aren't there more women? In *Competition Forum* (Vol. 17, No. 2, pp. 275–280). American Society for Competitiveness.

CMB & EBRD. (2020, September). *Capital Markets Board of Turkey Corporate Governance Monitoring Report 2019*. Capital Markets Board of Turkey. Retrieved May 10, 2022, from www.cmb.gov.tr/Sayfa/Dosya/115

Colakoglu, N., Eryilmaz, M., & Martínez-Ferrero, J. (2021). Is board diversity an antecedent of corporate social responsibility performance in firms? A research on the 500 biggest Turkish companies. *Social Responsibility Journal*, 17(2), 243–262. https://doi.org/10.1108/SRJ-07-2019-0251

Collins, C., Landivar, L. C., Ruppanner, L., & Scarborough, W. J. (2020). COVID-19 and the gender gap in work hours. *Gender, Work & Organisation*, 28, 101–112. https://doi.org/10.1111/gwao.12506

Conyon, M. J., & He, L. (2017). Firm performance and boardroom gender diversity: A quantile regression approach. *Journal of Business Research*, 79, 198–211. https://doi.org/10.1016/j.jbusres.2017.02.006

Di Stasio, V., & Larsen, E. N. (2020). The racialized and gendered workplace: Applying an intersectional lens to a field experiment on hiring discrimination in five European labor markets. *Social Psychology Quarterly*, 83(3), 229–250. https://doi.org/10.1177/0190272520902994

Döğer, N. (2022). *Ekonomik büyüme ve kadın işgücü arasındaki ilişki: Turkey için ampirik bir analiz* [The Relationship Between Economic Growth and Female Workforce: An Empirical Analysis for Turkey] [Master's thesis, Bursa Uludağ University]. Bursa Uludağ University Research Repository.

Ely, R., & Thomas, D. (2001). Cultural diversity at work: The effects of diversity perspectives on work group. *Administrative Science Quarterly*, 46(2), 229–273. https://doi.org/10.2307/2667087

European Commission (2020a). *A union of equality: Gender equality strategy 2020–2025*, COM (2020) 152 final, Brussels. Retreived from https://eur-lex.europa.eu/legal-content/EN/TXT/HTML/?uri=CELEX:52020DC0152&from=EN

EWOB. (2021). *Gender diversity index of women on boards and in corporate leadership*. EWOB. Retrieved May 29, 2022, from https://europeanwomenonboards.eu/wp-content/uploads/2022/01/2021-Gender-Diversity-Index.pdf

Greene, A. M., & Kirton, G. (2004). *Views from Another Stakeholder: Trade Union Perspectives on the Rhetoric of 'Managing Diversity'*. Industrial Relations Research Unit, Warwick Business School.
Grönlund, A., & Öun, I. (2018). In search of family-friendly careers? Professional strategies, work conditions and gender differences in work – family conflict. *Community, Work & Family*, 21(1), 87–105. https://doi.org/10.1080/13668803.2017.1375460
Hanzl, L., & Rehm, M. (2021). *Less Work, More Labour: School Closures and Work Hours During the COVID-19 Pandemic in Austria*. Ifso Working Paper. Retrieved from www.econstor.eu/handle/10419/233477
Holman, L., Stuart-Fox, D., & Hauser, C. E. (2018). The gender gap in science: How long until women are equally represented? *PLoS Biology*, 16(4), e2004956. https://doi.org/10.1371/journal.pbio.2004956
Hyrynsalmi, S., & Sutinen, E. (2019, June). *The Role of Women Software Communities in Attracting More Women to the Software Industry*. IEEE International Conference on Engineering, Technology and Innovation (ICE/ITMC) (pp. 1–7). Retrieved from https://ieeexplore.ieee.org/document/8792673
Ibsen, C. L., & Tapia, M. (2017). Trade union revitalisation: Where are we now? Where to next? *Journal of Industrial Relations*, 59(2), 170–191. https://doi.org/10.1177/0022185616677558
İnce, M., Gül, H., & Korkmaz, O. (2015). Çalışanların farklılıkların yönetimine ilişkin algılarında demografik değişkenlerin etkisi: Özel sektörde bir araştırma [The effect of demographic variables on employees' perceptions on diversity management: A study in the private sector]. *Niğde Üniversitesi İktisadi ve İdari Bilimler Fakültesi Dergisi*, 8(3), 111–126. Retrieved from https://dergipark.org.tr/en/pub/niguiibfd/issue/19759/211541
Isaacs, N., Lynch, I., Shabangu, C., Reygan, F., & Neluheni, M. (2020). Women in their full diversity? Provincial government responses to socio-economic exclusion of lesbian, bisexual and transgender women in Gauteng. *Agenda*, 34(1), 77–86. https://doi.org/10.1080/10130950.2019.1690323
Jackson, A. (2022). *Addressing Australia's Critical Skill Shortages: Unlocking Women's Economic Participation*. Retrieved from http://hdl.voced.edu.au/10707/610355
Joecks, J., Pull, K., & Vetter, K. (2013). Gender diversity in the boardroom and firm performance: What exactly constitutes a "critical mass?" *Journal of Business Ethics*, 118(1), 61–72. http://www.jstor.org/stable/42921212
Karayel, M., & Doğan, M. (2016). Board composition and firm performance: Evidence from BIST 100 companies in Turkey. *Economics and Applied Informatics*, 2, 33–40. Retrieved from https://ideas.repec.org/a/ddj/fseeai/y2016i2p33-40.html
Kevser, M. (2020). Farklılıkların yönetimi kavramına yönelik kuramsal bir değerlendirme *[A theoretical evaluation of the concept of diversity management]. International Journal of Business and Economic Studies*, 1 (2) , 86–95 . Retrieved from https://dergipark.org.tr/en/pub/uiecd/issue/52502/66866
Kılıç, M. (2015). The effect of board diversity on the performance of banks: Evidence from Turkey. *International Journal of Business and Management*, 10(9), 182. Retrieved from www.ccsenet.org/journal/index.php/ijbm/article/view/48944
Kirton, G., & Greene, A. M. (2022). *The Dynamics of Managing Diversity and Inclusion: A Critical Approach*. Routledge.

Kirton, G., & Greene, A.-M. (2004). *The Dynamics of Managing Diversity* (2nd ed.). Routledge. https://doi.org/10.4324/9780080468600

Kochan, T., Bezrukova, K., Ely, R., Jackson, S., Joshi, A., Jehn, K., . . . & Thomas, D. (2003). The effects of diversity on business performance: Report of the diversity research network. *Human Resource Management*, 42(1), 3–21. https://doi.org/10.1002/hrm.10061

Koç Holding Company. (n.d.). *Koç Holding: Diversity and Inclusion*. Koç Holding Company. Retrieved January 12, 2021, from www.koc.com.tr/sustainability/empower-people-together/inclusion-and-diversity

Küçükaltan, E. G., Hazarhun, E., & Müdüroğlu, G. (2020). Çalışanların işyerinde LGBTİ+ romantik ilişkilerine bakış açıları [Employees' perspectives on LGBTI+ romantic relationships in the workplace]. *Akdeniz İnsani Bilimler Dergisi*, 10(0), 229–246. https://doi.org/10.13114/MJH.2020.529

Küskü, F., Aracı, Ö., & Özbilgin, M. F. (2021). What happens to diversity at work in the context of a toxic triangle? Accounting for the gap between discourses and practices of diversity management. *Human Resource Management Journal*, 31(2), 553–574. https://doi.org/10.1111/1748-8583.12324

Larkey, L. K. (1996). Toward a Theory of Communicative Interactions in Culturally Diverse Workgroups. *The Academy of Management Review*, 21(2), 463–491. https://doi.org/10.2307/258669

Mavi. (n.d.). *Mavi'nin yönetim kurulunda çeşitlilik kapsamına giren temel prensipler* [Basic Principles within the Scope of Diversity in Mavi's Board of Directors]. Mavi P.C. Retrieved March 14, 2022, from www.mavicompany.com/i/assets/documents/pdf/2021/yonetim-kurulunda-cesitlilik-politikasi-2.pdf

Ngwakwe, C. (2020). Gender equality and extreme poverty alleviation in Sub-Saharan Africa. *Demography and Social Economy*, 42(4), 56–70. Retrieved from https://dse.org.ua/ojs/index.php/dse/article/view/14

Nelson, R., Sendroiu, I., Dinovitzer, R., & Dawe, M. (2019). Perceiving Discrimination: Race, Gender, and Sexual Orientation in the Legal Workplace. *Law & Social Inquiry*, 44(4), 1051–1082. doi:10.1017/lsi.2019.4

Noland, M., Moran, T., & Kotschwar, B. R. (2016). *Is Gender Diversity Profitable? Evidence from a Global Survey*. Peterson Institute for International Economics Working Paper (16–3). Retrieved from www.piie.com/publications/working-papers/gender-diversity-profitable-evidence-global-survey

Nunez-Smith, M., Pilgrim, N., Wynia, M., Desai, M. M., Jones, B. A., Bright, C., . . . & Bradley, E. H. (2009). Race/ethnicity and workplace discrimination: Results of a national survey of physicians. *Journal of General Internal Medicine*, 24(11), 1198–1204. https://doi.org/10.1007/s11606-009-1103-9

Oerlemans, W. G. M., Peeters, M. C. W., & Schaufeli, W. B. (2008). Ethnic diversity at work: An overview of theories and research. In Näswall, K., Hellgren, J., & Sverke, M. (Eds.), *The Individual in the Changing Working Life* (pp. 211–232). Cambridge University Press.

European Commission, Joint Research Centre, Haq, G., Ortega Hortelano, A., Tsakalidis, A. (2019). Women in European transport with a focus on research and innovation : an overview of women's issues in transport based on the Transport Research and Innovation Monitoring and Information System (TRI-

MIS), *Publications Office* of the European Union. https://data.europa.eu/doi/10.2760/08493

Osseo-Asare, A., Balasuriya, L., Huot, S. J., Keene, D., Berg, D., Nunez-Smith, M., . . . & Boatright, D. (2018). Minority resident physicians' views on the role of race/ethnicity in their training experiences in the workplace. *JAMA Network Open*, 1(5). https://doi.org/10.1001/jamanetworkopen.2018.2723

Otluoğlu, E., Sarı, E., & Çakmak, K. O. (2016). Yönetim kurulu çeşitliliğinin finansal performansa etkisi: Bist 100 üzerine bir araştırma [The impact of board diversity on financial performance: An evidence on BIST 100]. *Uluslararası Sosyal Araştırmalar Dergisi*, 9–46. Retrieved from https://ssrn.com/abstract=2884702

Özbilgin, M. (2015). Farklılık Yonetimi: Özel Sayıya Giriş. *Yönetim Araştırmaları Dergisi.* 12(1–2), 7. Retrieved from http://yad.baskent.edu.tr/files/2015_cilt_12.pdf

Özgünlü, F. (2019). *Çalışma yaşamında ayrımcılık: LGBT'lere yönelik bir araştırma* [Discrimination at Work Life: A Research of LGBT] [Master's thesis, Beykent University]. Beykent University Research Repository.

Özkaya, M. O., Özbilgin, M., & Şengül, C. M. (2008). Türkiye'de farklılıkların yönetimi: Türk ve yabancı ortaklı şirket örnekleri [Managing diversity in Turkey: Examples of Turkish and foreign partnership companies]. *Selçuk Üniversitesi Sosyal Bilimler Enstitüsü Dergisi*, 19, 359. Retrieved from https://dergipark.org.tr/en/pub/susbed/issue/61795/924253

Özsoy, Z., Şenyücel, M., & Oba, B. (2019, July 4–6). Gender diversity practices, in search of equality or window dressing? [Paper Presentation]. *35th European Group for Organisational Studies Colloquium*. Edinburgh.

Öztürk, M. B. (2011). Sexual orientation discrimination: Exploring the experiences of lesbian, gay and bisexual employees in Turkey. *Human Relations*, 64(8), 1099–1118. https://doi.org/10.1177/0018726710396249

Palmer, L., Matsick, J. L., Stevens, S. M., & Kuehrmann, E. (2021). Sexual orientation and gender influence perceptions of disciplinary fit: Implications for sexual and gender diversity in STEM. *Analyses of Social Issues and Public Policy*, 22(1), 315–337. https://doi.org/10.1111/asap.12290

Perry-Jenkins, M., & Gerstel, N. (2020). Work and family in the second decade of the 21st century. *Journal of Marriage and Family*, 82(1), 420–453. https://doi.org/10.1111/jomf.12636

SHRM. (2022). *Managing Flexible Work Arrangements*. Retrieved from www.shrm.org/resourcesandtools/tools-and-samples/toolkits/pages/managingflexiblework-arrangements.aspx

SPK. (2014). *Sermaye Piyasası Kurulu 2014 Faaliyet Raporu.* Sermaye Piyasası Kurulu. Retrieved from https://spk.gov.tr/data/61e48f651b41c60d1404d687/6c56f281d52e2a971f76c8c7c8d6845c.pdf

Sürgevil, O., & Budak, G. (2008). İşletmelerin farklılıkların yönetimi anlayışına yaklaşım tarzlarının saptanmasına yönelik bir araştırma [A research on determining approaches to management of diversity in businesses]. *Dokuz Eylül Üniversitesi Sosyal Bilimler Enstitüsü Dergisi*, 10(4), 65–96. Retrieved from https://arastirmax.com/en/system/files/dergiler/591/makaleler/10/4/arastirmax-isletmelerin-farkliliklarin-yonetimi-anlayisina-yaklasim-tarzlarinin-saptanmasina-yonelik-bir-arastirma.pdf

Tatli, A. (2011). A multi-layered exploration of the diversity management field: Diversity discourses, practices and practitioners in the UK. *British Journal of Management*, 22(2), 238–253. https://doi.org/10.1111/j.1467-8551.2010.00730.x

Terjesen, S., Couto, E.B. & Francisco, P.M. (2016). Does the presence of independent and female directors impact firm performance? A multi-country study of board diversity. *J Manag Gov* 20, 447–483. https://doi.org/10.1007/s10997-014-9307-8

Toossi, M., & Morisi, T. L. (2017). BLS spotlight on statistics: Women in the workforce before, during, and after the Great Recession. *U.S. Bureau of Labor Statistics*. Retrieved from www.bls.gov/spotlight/2017/women-in-the-workforce-before-during-and-after-the-great-recession/home.htm

Tozkoparan, G., & Vatansever, Ç. (2011). Farklılıkların yönetimi: İnsan kaynakları yöneticilerinin farklılık algısı üzerine bir odak grup çalışması [Diversity management: A focus group study of perception of diversity among human resource managers]. *Akdeniz Üniversitesi İktisadi ve İdari Bilimler Fakültesi Dergisi*, 21, 89–109. Retrieved from https://dergipark.org.tr/en/pub/auiibfd/issue/32324/359211

Tsui, A. S., Egan, T. D., & O'Reilly, C. A. (1992). Being Different: Relational Demography and Organizational Attachment. Administrative Science Quarterly, 37(4), 549–579. https://doi.org/10.2307/2393472

Usta, Ç Ö., & Bayraktar, O. (2017). İşletmelerde farklılıkların yönetimi ve işten ayrılma niyetine etkisi [Management of diversity in businesses and its effect on intention to leave]. *İş'te Davranış Dergisi*, 2(2), 68–78 . https://doi.org/10.25203/idd.327141

Wiley, C., & Monllor-Tormos, M. (2018). Board Gender Diversity in the STEM&F Sectors: The Critical Mass Required to Drive Firm Performance. Journal of Leadership & Organizational Studies, 25(3), 290–308. https://doi.org/10.1177/1548051817750535

World Economic Forum. (2021). *Global Gender Gap Report 2021*. Retrieved from www.weforum.org/reports/global-gender-gap-report-2021

Yağlı, İ., & Ünlü, U. (2019). Yönetim kurulu çeşitliliğinin firma değerine etkisi: Türkiye örneği [The effect of the diversity of the board of directors on the firm value: The case of Turkey]. *Mehmet Akif Ersoy Üniversitesi İktisadi ve İdari Bilimler Fakültesi Dergisi*, 6(1), 77–91. https://doi.org/10.30798/makuiibf.441797

Yeşil, S., & Pürtaş, S. (2017). Farklılıkların yönetimi, kurumsal itibar ve işletme performansı üzerine etkileri: Tekstil sektöründe bir alan araştırması [The effects of diversity management on corporate reputation and firm performance: A field study in textile industry]. *Kahramanmaraş Sütçü İmam Üniversitesi İktisadi ve İdari Bilimler Fakültesi Dergisi*, 7(2), 173–194. Retrieved from http://iibfdergisi.ksu.edu.tr/en/pub/issue/33603/372960

Yildirim, T. M.; & Eslen-Ziya, H. (2021). The differential impact of COVID-19 on the work conditions of women and men academics during the lockdown. *Gender, Work and Organization*, 28, 243–249. https://doi.org/10.1111/gwao.12529

Yıldız, S., Meydan, C., Taştan Boz, İ., & Sakal, Ö. (2019). Do the quota applications for women on Boards improve financial performance. *Sustainability*, 11(21), 5901. https://doi.org/10.3390/su11215901

Young, M., & Schieman, S. (2018). Scaling back and finding flexibility: Gender differences in parents' strategies to manage work – family conflict. *Journal of Marriage and Family*, 80(1), 99–118. https://doi.org/10.1111/jomf.12435

2 The Turkish context

One foot forward, two steps back

Introduction

The diversity management landscape in Turkey is characterised by the divergences between rhetoric and practice and the state as the dominant actor in shaping the behaviour of firms in the adoption and implementation of relevant practices.

Extant research on the attitudes of various groups of employees (for example, human resources managers and career counsellors) about diversity management provides evidence that "diversity" in the workplace is conceptualised as incorporating differences in gender, race, ethnicity, sexual orientation, age, physical capabilities, disability, culture, nationality, social class, political association, ex-offenders, occupation, and place of birth (Usta & Bayraktar, 2017; Bozkurt et al., 2013; İnce et al., 2015; Tozkoparan & Vatansever, 2011). In these studies, academicians and practitioners employ a similar rhetoric that reflects a broad conceptualisation of diversity. On the other hand, research on the practices adopted by companies for diversity management showed that the majority of them mainly adhered to legal requirements (Yeşil & Pürtaş, 2017; Sürgevil & Budak, 2008) and lacked awareness of diversity and its management (Sürgevil & Budak, 2008). For example, the Sürgevil and Budak (2008) study indicated that companies conceptualise diversity in relation to age, gender, disability, and ex-offender which in turn is in accord with the labour laws. The same study also stated that companies do not implement diversity management since there is not a pressure from investors, the state, or rivals to do so. Another study focusing on the diversity management practices of domestic and foreign firms in Turkey (Özkaya et al., 2008) reported similar results: Domestic and foreign firms showed similar tendencies in gender diversity practices, that is, management cadres were male dominated, and both groups of companies implemented the legally required quotas for disabled, ex-offenders, and victims of terror. However, they all employed less than the legally set ratio, and

DOI: 10.4324/9781003244868-3

they engaged in such a recruitment policy due to legal obligations. Given the results of extant studies, we can say that in the Turkish context, diversity is narrowed down to "gender diversity" and diversity management is understood as compliance with labour laws. Race, ethnicity, and sexual orientation are still taboo issues (Sürgevil & Budak, 2008; Öztürk, 2011). Furthermore, based on the extant research that highlighted the practices of companies and relying on the work of Lombardo et al. (2010), we can argue that the Turkish business community "bends" the meaning of diversity management to "gender diversity" and instrumentalises it for image and reputation building.

In Turkey, diversity and inclusion in the workplace are especially important in relation to women, who still encounter numerous discriminatory practices. For instance, the Global Gender Gap Report (World Economic Forum, 2021) highlighted the deepening gender gap in Turkey: High rates of unemployment for women, high rates of part-time employment for women, low rates of employment of women in top management positions, and low representation on boards of directors. Women's higher education is not translated into higher labour force participation, women are underrepresented in management and leadership roles (Aycan, 2004; World Economic Forum, 2021), women tend to earn less than men for equal work (ILO, 2020), and women opt out of the workforce to a much higher degree than men (Akhmedjonov, 2012).

Furthermore, despite the worldwide initiatives to increase gender diversity in corporate life, in Turkey, various actors – the state, business, business associations, and unions – are disinclined to draft and implement the necessary measures. Therefore, in the following section, we will focus on cultural and political factors that shape women's inclusion in the workplace. In so doing, we will focus on the historical interplay between the dominant actors (the state, listed companies, and the EU) and contextual factors (culture and politics) in shaping practices related to gender diversity in Turkey.

Politics of gender in(equality)

In the early years of the Turkish Republic, legal reforms were enacted to ensure gender equality in political and civil rights. In 1934, Turkish women obtained the right to vote, and they could be elected to the Turkish Grand National Assembly (Tekeli, 1993). In 1937, secularism was explicitly mentioned in the second article of the then-Turkish constitution, which ensured that the country's secular nature could not be changed or even proposed to be changed. Through secularism, Turkish women obtained civil rights and social norms that in the past had constrained them from full participation in the economic and social sphere (Özbilgin et al., 2011). During this period, while women attained more political rights (Arat, 1989; Kandiyoti,

2019) and visibility in the public sphere (Coşar & Yeğenoğlu, 2011), the cultural norms of Turkish society that shaped gender relations and sexuality persisted. In the process of acquiring political rights – called "state sponsored feminism" by Kandiyoti (1988, 2019) – Turkish women were "emancipated but not liberated" (Toprak, 1990) since the legal regulations then constituted reflected patriarchal premises that perceived women's primary roles as wives and mothers (Kandiyoti, 1988; White, 2003; Tekeli, 1986). Thus, on the one hand, Republican reforms on gender issues expanded the public roles assumed by women but, on the other hand, they reinforced and even legitimised the traditional social roles attributed to women (Arat, 1989, 2005). During this period, labour force participation by women was limited, and only a few women with a university education joined the labour market, mainly as professionals (Toksöz, 2012; Gündüz-Hoşgör & Smits, 2008; Öncü, 1981; Erkut, 1982). In other words, although the presence of women in professions such as doctors, lawyers, teachers, and academicians was high, they had a far lower presence in the labour market or political realm than men (Kandiyoti, 2019).

Women's participation in the labour force was visible in rural, agricultural areas, where they worked as unpaid family workers of small commodity producers (Toksöz, 2016). In the 1950s, with the shift of government policies from traditional farming to mechanisation in agriculture (Aydın, 2010), rural class structure went through a major transformation; small producers migrated to the peripheries of big cities and formed an informal labour force (Değirmenci, 2021; Aydın, 2010). During this transition and massive migration wave, in line with the premises of the patriarchal society, men assumed the breadwinner roles while women's role was limited to household chores (Toksöz, 2012). The uneducated women, who used to have some economic independence as unpaid family workers, were transformed into full-time housewives or were limited to positions in the low-paying urban informal economy (Erman, 1998).

One of the major transformations in Turkish political, economic, and social history was the initiation of the structural adjustment program and the military coup d'état of 12 September 1980. The then-governing party, Anavatan Parti (ANAP), initiated the implementation of a structural adjustment program based on the recommendations of the WB, and the neoliberal turn in the economy started. While the structural adjustment program marked a major shift in the economic policies, the coup marked a juncture in politics, with "an official transition from secularism to religion-based nationalism" (Kandiyoti, 2019, p. 139), and in the social structure of society, with the formation of a conservative neoliberal understanding of patriarchy – the familial patriarch. Accordingly, the place of women in society was confined to the realm of family. In the economic realm, with the proscription of trade union activities by the coup, real wages were lowered. With the implementation of the export-led industrialisation policy in line with the neoliberal policies, employment rates declined in most industries, except textiles and food processing (Toksöz, 2011). Consequently, women's participation in the labour force was more for temporary jobs, and the preference of the employers was more for single and young women. Married women, especially those with children, were excluded by employers because of their childcare responsibilities. They were also excluded because the turnover among married women was higher than it was among single women, because it was difficult for married women to cope with the demanding working conditions and house chores. As discussed by Toksöz (2012), this situation – the exclusion of married women from the labour force – reveals "a collaboration between patriarchy and the capitalist economy" (p. 69).

After the 1980 military coup, a strong feminist movement emerged, led by educated, secular women, mainly supporters of leftist ideas (Kandiyoti, 2019; Coşar & Yeğenoğlu, 2011). The movement raised public awareness of the violations of women's rights and initiated a broad struggle base for more egalitarian and less patriarchal legal adjustments (Arat, 2016). The women's movement in Turkey strengthened in the 1990s, and Turkish women gained much more power in public institutions, universities, and civil society. International agreements and the process of EU accession facilitated a milieu where governments were obliged to draft policies that enabled more inclusive participation of women in the labour force and helped feminist attempts to promote the rights of women in reference to human rights. The Convention on the Elimination of All Forms of Discrimination against Women (CEDAW), which proposed positive discrimination measures for women, was endorsed in 1985. As required by CEDAW, in 1991 a governmental body – the General Directorate of Women's Status and Problems – was established as the overseer of gender equality. During the 1990s, laws were approved to eliminate discrimination against women, and a law to protect survivors of domestic violence was ratified in 1998. Through the Helsinki European summit in 1999 that granted Turkey the status of official candidate for membership in the EU, Turkey updated its fundamental laws with respect to gender equality, enacting constitutional amendments in 2001, 2004, and 2010 and adopting a new civil code in 2001 and a new penal code in 2004. In the economic realm, a reform process was initiated to harmonise Turkey's existing legislation and practices with the EU requirements in terms of gender equality in employment. Also, the position of women independent from family and children was recognised in official documents. Although this process brought positive changes for women, many issues were left unaddressed. Since women's perspectives were underrepresented during the legislation process, some problems, such as sexist attitudes, persisted (Bakırcı, 2010). The legislation on employment, discrimination, health, and safety in the workplace was not harmonised with EU standards. The commission's progress reports noted that the community directives concerning discrimination on the grounds of gender, racial or ethnic origin, religion or belief, disability, age, or sexual orientation were incomplete (Bakırcı, 2010).

In the 2002 elections, the Justice and Development Party (AKP), which was founded by a younger generation of the early Islamist parties, obtained 34.3 percent of the votes and came into power as a single party. The majority of Turkish citizens at that time, along with the social democrats and even the AKP's primary constituency of the Muslim right, supported the integration into the EU project (Arat, 2001) and declared a liberal party agenda which even promised to uphold CEDAW (Arat, 2016; Arat, 2010; Kandiyoti, 2019; Ün, 2019). In its first term, the AKP government, in line with the EU accession process, drafted legislative changes. During the course of developing these legislations, women's NGOs that were formed after the 1980s had an influential role in lobbying for gender-sensitive issues. However, this cooperation between the government and the women's NGOs did not last long since the AKP changed its stance and started to employ a conservative rhetoric coupled with the implementation of neoliberal policies in the economic realm. The rhetoric shifted from "gender equality" to the importance of women for the protection of "family". The societal role of women was limited to child rearing, taking care of the elderly, and creating a happy family life. Similarly, "discrimination of women" was replaced by "protection of women". The focus on family rather than women and hostility towards feminist movements were frequently displayed by the AKP cadres. For example, in 2014 at the First International Summit for Women and Justice, Prime Minister Recep Tayyip Erdoğan stated,

> Women and men cannot be treated equally because it goes against the laws of nature. Their characters, habits and physiques are different. You cannot place a mother breastfeeding her baby on an equal footing with men. You cannot make women work in the same jobs as men do. . . . This is against their delicate nature. Our religion has defined a position for women: motherhood.
>
> (Cumhuriyet, 2014)

This shift in rhetoric was not only openly stated by political leaders, but it was also incorporated into the official documents of the government. For example, in the 10th Development Plan, women's issues were addressed under the heading of "Women and Family" and gender equality was mentioned as the empowerment of women for the improvement of the status of the family (Toksöz, 2016, p. 77). This shift in rhetoric was reflected in the implementations of the government. The General Directorate of Women's Status and Problems, which was initiated as a prerequisite of CEDAW, was abolished in 2011, and in its place, the Ministry of the Family and Social Policies was established. As a countermove to the existing women's NGOs, pro-government, government-initiated NGOs were activated under the scrutiny of the Turkish Family Platform (TURAP) (http://turkiyeaileplatformu.com/).

Furthermore, through various welfare reforms, women were distanced from the labour market and relegated to the household for the happiness of the family. One such example was the Conditional Cash Transfer (CCT) program endorsed by the WB. In line with the premises of the program, mothers living in poverty were supported with cash for health checks and schooling expenses of their children (Bergman & Tafolar, 2014; Şener, 2016). On paper, the program seemed to be aimed at the empowerment of the women; however, it was structured in such a way that women were taken not as active participants in the labour market but as caregivers (Şener, 2019). Furthermore, CCTs were instrumentalised by the AKP for reinforcing its political power by emphasising the benevolence of the AKP cadres (Bergman & Tafolar, 2014). As women were encouraged to stay at home and take care of their families, they were more and more positioned as informal workers in textiles, food processing, and services industries either as self-employed petit entrepreneurs or workers (Toksöz, 2016). The modest incomes generated in these informal setting are usually considered contributions to the betterment of the family budget and as providing an opportunity for women to have enough time to carry out their housework. Another example of moving women back to the home is the grant (the amount is close to minimum wage) given to those who take care of disabled people in low-income households. Since 2007, these grants have been allocated by the Ministry of Family and Social Policies and are mainly received by women (Tokgöz, 2016) and those who are not covered by the social security system.

In line with the neoliberal policies followed by the government, a new labour law (No. 4857) was drafted in 2003. With this new legislation, flexible work, part-time work, temporary jobs, and subcontracting were legalised (Ercan & Oğuz, 2014; Özdemir & Yücesan-Özdemir, 2006). These issues were presented with rhetoric that encouraged women to be part of the labour force without abandoning their traditional roles as mothers and caregivers (Oğuz, 2020). In addition, the financial burden of establishing childcare facilities in the workplace was shifted to the women employees who were engaged in part-time work. Such implementations, especially with the enfeeblement of labour unions, put women in a precarious position. That is, women were the first to be laid off in times of crises, and they worked without full social security coverage (Toksöz, 2016). The law was also instrumental in introducing dire working conditions because it subordinated workers, giving employers the discretion to determine the working conditions – such as allocating weekly working hours, determining starting/ending times and break times, and protecting children and pregnant women – and the right to lay off employees. We think that the following case, compiled from newspaper articles, illustrates the conditions faced by women workers and the positions taken by employers and unions in a local company.

> DSL is a seafood processing company and during the week of the 8th of March (women's day in Turkey), its advertisements appeared on all national TV channels at primetime. The slogan of these advertisements was "What makes DSL is the labour of our women workers"; "It's not men who made DSL, its women who made DSL the most reliable company, its women behind DSL's exports". The company was proud to announce that women comprised most of its labour force and women of different ages were saying, "DSL is our home, DSL is everything to us".
>
> More or less around the same some social media accounts and newspapers started to uncover the working conditions of women in DSL. During the pandemic the company started to implement a "closed circuit work system" where dressing rooms and toilets are monitored by cameras, in most of the cases they are locked and talking to each other is forbidden in the factory. A working day is 9 hours 30 minutes and workers are given only one break – 30 minutes and for lunch. Checking the time from the telephone is a reason to reduce their wage. They work without social security coverage; turnover rates are very high, and a worker is usually dismissed within four months. If they show an interest in a labour union, they are threatened with being seen as infamous in the eyes of their husbands, fathers, or neighbours. One interviewee also mentioned that a women worker was exposed to the violence of a foreman, she made a complaint to the management, and she was fired with an accusation that the foreman's manhood pride was damaged.
>
> Unions are still silent, mainstream media is silent, women's platforms and alternative media actively voice the issue. The company improved its financial position by increasing its sales revenue and annual profits.

Conclusion

The diversity management landscape in Turkey can be explained in relation to the tropes of patriarchal culture and state dominance in the cultivation and preservation of these norms. Gender equality has always been a domain of conflicting ideals and tensions between conservative and modernist constituencies in Turkey. While the main argument of conservatives is about the weakening of traditional values regarding sex roles, the modernists favour women's rights and equality. Thus, women face barriers in the domain of work as there is an inherent conflict between the prevailing traditional sex roles and the roles they must play in the contemporary workplace (Arat, 2010; Dildar, 2015). Traditional gender roles ascribe dominance, independence, and leadership capability to men while assigning dependency, submissiveness, and caregiving (child and elderly) to women (Sakallı-Ugurlu & Beydogan, 2002). In Turkey, men and women grow up believing that they must live up to the expectations of the idealised gender roles culturally prescribed by society. Patriarchy and sexism can lead to discrimination against women in the workplace since they promulgate negative attitudes towards women. Furthermore, because of internalisation of patriarchal norms, women willingly withdraw from work life. Instead, they prefer being the "mistress of their own house" (Dildar, 2015, p. 53).

Given the dominance of patriarchal norms, the governing cadres instrumentalised gender equality as a pivot to balance electoral support. Gender equality was taken as gaining political rights and participation in the public sphere during the early days of the Republic. However, the traditional roles assigned to women persevered. In the late 1990s, with the drive of international treaties, EU accession, and women's movement organisations, more inclusive policies for women were drafted. However, this positive wave was interrupted by the implementation of neoliberal policies and the conservative attitude of the AKP government. From then on, gender equality was supplanted by gender justice. The trope of patriarchy replaced gender equality with familism. The presence of women in the labour force has been marginalised to temporary jobs without social security coverage. Instead, the place of women has been limited to "house" where they can perform caregiver roles. As the governments became more committed to implementing the tools (such as flexible, temporary work) of a neoliberal economy, instrumentalising welfare reforms that distance women from paid labour, and adhering to the norms of patriarchy for securing votes, the gender gap will deepen and gender diversity in the workplace will be an unattainable ideal farfetched appeal.

References

Akhmedjonov, A. (2012). New evidence on pay gap between men and women in Turkey. *Economics Letters*, 117(1), 32–34. https://doi.org/10.1016/j.econlet.2012.04.070

Arat, Y. (1989). *The Patriarchal Paradox: Women Politicians in Turkey*. Fairleigh Dickinson University Press.

Arat, Y. (2001). 'Women's rights as human rights: The Turkish case'. *Human Rights Review, 3:*1, 27-34. https://doi.org/10.1007/s12142-001-1003-9

Arat, Y. (2005). Gender and citizenship in Turkey, in Moghissi, H. (ed.) *Women and Islam: Critical Concepts in Sociology*, Routledge, London, 58–70.

Arat, Y. (2010). Religion, politics and gender equality in Turkey: Implications of a democratic paradox? *Third World Quarterly*, 31(6), 869–884. Retrieved from www.jstor.org/stable/27896586

Arat, Y. 2016. Islamist women and feminist concerns in vontemporary Turkey: Prospects for women's rights and solidarity. *Frontiers: A Journal of Women Studies, 37*(3), 125–150. https://doi.org/10.5250/fronjwomestud.37.3.0125

Arat, Y. (2021), "Democratic backsliding and the instrumentalization of women's rights in Turkey", *Politics & Gender*, 1–31. https://doi.org/10.1017/S1743923X21000192

Aycan, Z. (2004). Key success factors for women in management in Turkey. *Applied Psychology*, 53(3), 453–477. https://doi.org/10.1111/j.1464-0597.2004.00180.x

Aydın, Z. (2010). Neo-liberal transformation of Turkish agriculture", *Journal of Agrarian Change*, 10(2): 149–187. https://doi.org/10.1111/j.1471-0366.2009.00241.x

Bakırcı, K. (2010). Gender equality in employment in Turkish legislation with comparisons to EU and international law. *Journal of Workplace Rights.* 15(1), 3–25. Retrieved from https://access.portico.org/Portico/auView?auId=ark:%2F27927%2Fpgk5szzgs5

Bergmann, C., & Tafolar, M. (2014) "Combating social inequalities in Turkey through conditional cash transfers (CCT)? (Conference Proceeding). *9th Global Labor University Conference "Inequality within and among Nations: Causes, Effects, and Responses"*. Berlin School of Economics and Law.

Bozkurt, S., Doğan, A., & Karaeminoğulları, A. (2013). An investigation of job and career counseling candidates from the perspective of diversity management. *Dokuz Eylül Üniversitesi Sosyal Bilimler Enstitüsü Dergisi,* 15(4), 589–606. Retrieved from http://acikerisim.deu.edu.tr:8080/xmlui/handle/20.500.12397/5308

Coşar, S., & Yeğenoğlu, M. (2011). New grounds for patriarchy in Turkey? Gender policy in the age of AKP. *South European Society and Politics*, 16(4), 555–573. https://doi.org/10.1080/13608746.2011.571919

Cumhuriyet (2014, November 24). *Erdoğan: Kadın ile erkeği eşit konuma getiremezsiniz, fitratına aykırı* [Erdogan: You Cannot Make Men and Women Equal, it is Against Their Nature]. Retrieved from www.cumhuriyet.com.tr/video/erdogan-kadin-ile-erkegi-esit-konuma-getiremezsiniz-fitratina-aykiri-148691

Değirmenci, S. (2021) *Türkiye'de tarım kapitalistleşirken; Talepler ve Yasalar [While agriculture capitalized in Turkey: Demands and legislation],* SAV Yayinları, İstanbul.

Dildar, Y. (2015). Patriarchal norms, religion, and female labour supply: Evidence from Turkey. *World Development*, 76, 40–61. https://doi.org/10.1016/j.worlddev.2015.06.010

Ercan, F., & Oğuz, Ş. (2014). Rethinking anti-neoliberal strategies through the perspective of value theory: Insights from the Turkish case. *Science and Society Quarterly*, 71(2). https://doi.org/10.1521/siso.2007.71.2.173

Erman, T. (1998). The impact of migration on Turkish rural women: Four emergent patterns. *Gender & Society*, *12*(2), 146–167. https://doi.org/10.1177/08912439801 20020

Erkut, S. (1982). Social psychology looks at but does not see the undergraduate woman. *The Undergraduate Woman: Issues in Educational Equity*, 103–204.

Gündüz-Hoşgör, A., & Smits, J. (2008). Variation in labor market participation of married women in Turkey. *Women's Studies International Forum*, 31(2), 104–117. https://doi.org/10.1016/j.wsif.2008.03.003

İnce, M., Gül, H., Çakıcı, A. B., & Candan, H. (2015). Örgütlerde sınırlandırıcı ya da sürükleyici güç olarak farklılıkların yönetimi [Management of diversity as a limiting or dragging force in organizations]. *Gümüşhane Üniversitesi Sosyal Bilimler Elektronik Dergisi*, 12, 3–30.

ILO. (2020). *Measuring the gender wage gap: Case of Turkey. International Labour Organisation.* Turkey Office and TurkStat. Retrieved from https://www.ilo.org/ankara/publications/WCMS_756660/lang--en/index.htm

Kandiyoti, D. (1988). Bargaining with patriarchy. *Gender and Society*, 2, 274–289.

Kandiyoti, D. (2009). Islam, modernity and the politics of gender, in Masud, M. K., Salvatore, A. and van Bruinessen (eds.), Islam and modernity: Key issues and debates, Edinburgh University Press, 91–124.

Kandiyoti, D. (2019). Against all odds: The resilience and fragility of women's gender activism in Turkey. In Kandiyoti, D., Al-Ali, N., & Poots, S. K. (Eds.), *Gender, Governance and Islam*. Edinburg University Press.

Lombardo, E., Meier, P., & Verloo, M. (2010). Discursive dynamics in gender equality politics: What about 'feminist taboos'?, *European Journal of Women's Studies*, 17(2), 105–123. https://doi.org/10.1177/1350506809359562

Oğuz, S. (2020). Türkiye'de yedek işgücü ordusu ve farklı biçimleri: Hane halkı işgüücü anketlerinden gözlemler, 2004–2013 [Reserve army labour and its different forms in Turkey: Household labour surveys, 2004–2013]. *Praksis*, 23, 141–170.

Öncü, A. (1981). Turkish Women in the Professions: Why so many? in Abadan-Unat, N., Kandiyoti, D. and Kıray, K. (eds.) *Women in Turkish Society*, EJ Brill, Leiden, 181–193.

Özdemir, A. M., & Yücesan-Özdemir, G. (2006). Labour law reform in Turkey in the 2000s: The devil is not in detail but in the legal texts too. *Economic and Industrial Democracy*, 27(2), 311–331.

Özbilgin, M., Syed, J., & Derili, B. 2011. Managing gender diversity in Pakistan and Turkey: a historical review. International Handbook on Diversity Management at Work, Edward Elgar, Cheltenham, 11–26.

Özkaya, M. O., Özbilgin, M., & Şengül, C. M. (2008). Türkiye'de farklılıkların yönetimi: Türk ve yabancı ortaklı şirket örnekleri [Managing diversity in Turkey: Examples of Turkish and foreign partnership companies]. *Selçuk Üniversitesi Sosyal Bilimler Enstitüsü Dergisi*, 19, 359. Retrieved from https://dergipark.org.tr/en/pub/susbed/issue/61795/924253

Öztürk, M. B. (2011). Sexual orientation discrimination: Exploring the experiences of lesbian, gay and bisexual employees in Turkey. *Human Relations*, 64(8), 1099–1118. https://doi.org/10.1177/0018726710396249

Sakalli-Ugurlu, N., & Beydogan, B. (2002). Turkish college students' attitudes toward women managers: The effects of patriarchy, sexism, and gender differences. *The Journal of Psychology: Interdisciplinary and Applied*, 136(6), 647–656. https://doi.org/10.1080/00223980209604825

Sürgevil, O., & Budak, G. (2008). İşletmelerin farklılıkların yönetimi anlayışına yaklaşım tarzlarının saptanmasına yönelik bir araştırma [A research on determining approaches to management of diversity in businesses]. *Dokuz Eylül Üniver-*

sitesi Sosyal Bilimler Enstitüsü Dergisi, 10(4), 65–96. Retrieved from https://arastirmax.com/en/system/files/dergiler/591/makaleler/10/4/arastirmax-isletmelerin-farkliliklarin-yonetimi-anlayisina-yaklasim-tarzlarinin-saptanmasina-yonelik-bir-arastirma.pdf

Şener, M. Y. (2016) "Conditional cash transfers in Turkey: A case to reflect on the AKP's approach to gender and social policy", *Research and Policy on Turkey*, 1(2): 164–178, https://doi.org/10.1080/23760818.2016.1201246

Tekeli, S. (1986). *Kadın bakışı açısından kadınlar: 1980'ler Türkiye'sinde kadınlar* [From the perspective of women, women in 1980's Turkey], İletişim Yayınları, İstanbul.

Toprak, B. 1990. *Emancipated but unliberated women in Turkey: The impact of Islam. Women,* Family and Social Change in Turkey, Bangkok: UNESCO.

Tozkoparan, G., & Vatansever, Ç. (2011). Farklılıkların yönetimi: İnsan kaynakları yöneticilerinin farklılık algısı üzerine bir odak grup çalışması [Diversity management: A focus group study of perception of diversity among human resource managers]. *Akdeniz Üniversitesi İktisadi ve İdari Bilimler Fakültesi Dergisi*, 21, 89–109. Retrieved from https://dergipark.org.tr/en/pub/auiibfd/issue/32324/359211

Toksöz, G. (2011). Women's employment in turkey in the light of different trajectories in development-different patterns in women's employment *Fe Dergi* 3(2), 19–32.

Toksöz, G. (2012) The state of female labor in the impasse of neoliberal market and patriarchal family and society, in Dedeoğlu, Saniye/Elveren, Adem (eds.), *Gender and society in Turkey: The impact of neo-liberal policies, political Islam and EU accession.* London/New York: I.B. Tairus, 47–65.

Toksöz, G. (2016). Transition from 'woman'to 'family': An analysis of AKP era employment policies from a gender perspective. *Journal für Entwicklungspolitik*, 32(1/2), 64–83.

Usta, Ö. Ç., & Bayraktar, O. (2017). İşletmelerde farklılıkların yönetimi ve işten ayrılma niyetine etkisi [Management of diversity in businesses and its effect on intention to leave]. *İş'te Davranış Dergisi*, 2(2), 68–78. https://doi.org/10.25203/idd.327141

Ün, M. B. (2019). Contesting global gender equality norms: the case of Turkey. *Review of International Studies*, 45(5), 828–847. https://doi.org/10.1017/S026021051900024X

World Economic Forum. (2021). *Global Gender Gap Report 2021*. Retrieved from www.weforum.org/reports/global-gender-gap-report-2021

White, J. B. (2003). State feminism, modernization, and the Turkish republican woman. *NWSA Journal*, 15(3), 145–159. http://www.jstor.org/stable/4317014

Yeşil, S., & Pürtaş, S. (2017). Farklılıkların yönetimi, kurumsal itibar ve işletme performansı üzerine etkileri: Tekstil sektöründe bir alan araştırması [The effects of diversity management on corporate reputation and firm performance: A field study in textile industry]. *Kahramanmaraş Sütçü İmam Üniversitesi İktisadi ve İdari Bilimler Fakültesi Dergisi*, 7(2), 173–194. Retrieved from http://iibfdergisi.ksu.edu.tr/en/pub/issue/33603/372960

3 The state

How to withdraw from responsibilities

Introduction

The state plays a dominant role in the introduction, shaping, and implementation of diversity programs in Turkey. In other words, the politics of gender diversity is mediated by legislation, discourse, and institutions in line with the political concerns of the ruling cadres. Similarly, a shift from a state-led industrialisation period to market-based liberalisation in 1980 and full-blown neoliberalisation after 2002 was instrumental in shaping the relations between different actors involved in the gender diversity field. The role of the state in this transformation process has been identified as "state sponsored feminism" (Kandiyoti, 1991) during the 1924–1980 period, the "vanguard" of the feminist movement between 1980–2010, and the instrumentalisation of women's rights by the government cadres after 2010 (Arat, 2021; Kandiyoti, 2019). The emphasis of the gender regime during these three periods changed from "women's rights" to "gender equality" and finally to "gender justice" (for details, see Tabak et al., 2022; Ün, 2019). Although the state has had a dominant role in whittling down the gender diversity regime, actors such as NGOs, women's platforms, international organisations, and publicly listed companies have contributed to the evolution of gender diversity practice through time. This is because the power relations between state cadres and these non-state organisations oscillated between disputation, backing, and co-optation where sovereignties are traded and alliances are built.

This chapter discusses the role of the state in the evolution of the gender diversity practices of listed companies. In so doing, we follow the periodisation done in Chapter 2 with a special emphasis on the changes in related legislation, discourse adopted, institutions developed, and the power relations between state and non-state actors. Since gender diversity initiatives gained momentum after 1980, we provide a deeper analysis of the second and third period based on changes in the economic and political regime. We aim to

DOI: 10.4324/9781003244868-4

show how the interests of the ruling government cadres in appropriating gender diversity talk and walk changed in tandem with the adoption of neo-liberal policies and a weak, "illiberal democracy". We see this process as the marginalization of gender diversity practices where women's status in society and in workplace is deliberately neglected in an authoritarian, populist political realm hosting neo-liberal employment policies. Furthermore, since gender diversity discourse and practices are influenced by the women's movement and the position taken by the state towards this movement's adherents, our analysis of gender diversity is aligned with the premises of the women's movement in each period.

From "women's rights" to "gender equality"

During the early years of the Republic, with a state-led, top-down process, women's rights with related legislation in participating to elections, education and labour market was secured. Primary education became mandatory, the Islamic civil code was changed, and women were granted the right to participate in the political realm. During the same period under the leadership of Nezihe Muhiddin, there was an initiative to establish the Turkish Women's Party (Türk Kadınlar Partisi) for the advocacy of women's active participation in politics. However, their application for legal status was rejected by the government officials (Kandiyoti, 2019; Sancar, 2012; Ecevit, 2007). Thus, the Turkish Women's Union (Türk Kadınlar Birliği) was established in 1924 as a non-state organisation for supporting women. Although the legislation, did not allow the Union to be involved in politics, enfranchisement had always been on its agenda. In this process, the relationship between the state and the sole women's organisation to opt for suffrage can be described as "co-optation" (Kandiyoti, 2019; Ecevit, 2007). Nevertheless, the Union achieved its aim, women's suffrage in 1935, which was supported by Kemalist reforms. The role of the state at this time was described by Ecevit (2007) as moulding the women's movement for its nation-building purposes, co-opting women in order to avoid an independent women's movement. Non-state actors struggling for women's rights complied with the directives provided by the state and assumed a philanthropic role (Sancar, 2012). This period of co-optation and silence continued until the 1980s with some variations.

At this point it is worth noting that, during the 1960 to 1980 period, there were non-state organisations advocating for women's rights in the workplace (including things such as childcare services and longer maternity leave) and opposing the civil code that assigned the family representative role to the husband and made the wife's workplace involvement subject to the permission of the husband (Ecevit, 2007). Even though the operations of the Union were finalised by the 1970 coup, other remarkable organisations were established during this period. Issues such as "maternity leave, equal pay for equal work, social security coverage for domestic workers and early retirement" (Ecevit, 2007, p. 194) for women were on the agenda of the Association of Progressive Women. This association organised campaigns, workshops, and forums to raise awareness among women workers in factories and to persuade women to be active within unions (Ecevit, 2007). The reaction of the government to the issues raised by these organisations can be described as deliberate neglect, and the organisations were kept under close surveillance. Finally, by the 1980 military coup, the operations of these organisations were banned.

The post-1980 era diverged from the abovementioned initiatives in relations between the state and non-state actors and included proliferation in the number and scope of non-state actors and issues regarding "gender equality". The period is notable for the implementation of a structural adjustment program on the economic realm, which included initiatives for gender diversity issues in line with the second feminist wave that prioritised "gender equality". The period witnessed mass demonstrations against domestic violence, sexual harassment, body politics, and unequal treatment in the courts that were mainly organised by left-oriented feminists (Kandiyoti, 2019). In line with the rising feminist movement, various national and international NGOs exerted pressure over the government for the elimination of discrimination against women. These pressures led to changes in legislation and the development of institutions. During this period, the relationship between state and non-state organisations was identified as "contestation and cooperation", a process where state agencies learned from the contesting groups how to promote gender equality.

The 1980s and 1990s were marked by the emergence and proliferation of NGOs promoting gender equality (Kandiyoti, 2019; Diner & Toktaş, 2010). The period witnessed the foundation of NGOs such as Mor Çati (offers shelter and protection for abused women), Uçan Süpürge (empowers women and ensures gender equality), and KA-DER (supports women's political representation) and platforms such as Solidarity Against Battering and Saturday Mothers. The women activists involved in these organisations were professionals (Ün, 2019) and were radical leftists or Kemalists (Tabak et al., 2022) in their political orientation. These organisations and the activists involved in them acted as forerunners of feminism. Their claims aligned with the global gender equality norms supported by international organisations. They forced the government to build institutions and draft legislation for gender equality. Accordingly, in 1986, the government ratified CEDAW. With the impetus of campaigns organised by activist groups, government cadres were forced to make changes in the criminal and civil code, and in 2001, they implemented the new civil code guaranteeing full equality between men and women. Under various amendments, women were given the right to participate in the labour force without the permission of their husbands, and violence in the family and harassment in the workplace were penalised (Ün, 2019).

Another stream of changes that underlined the gender politics of the period was the development of institutions by the state for promoting gender equality. In line with the promises of CEDAW and Turkey's EU accession process in 1990, the Directorate on the Status and Problems of Women and later a ministry for women and family were established. As a state organisation, the Directorate was responsive to the claims and ideas of the non-state women's organisations and tried to incorporate the suggestions and proposals of these groups into its plans, while providing input and advice to the state agencies. NGOs retained their critical stance in evaluating the state policies regarding women's issues. As described by Ecevit (2007), this was an "uneasy collaboration" with the state (p. 198). Other noteworthy examples of institutions developed during this period were women's studies centres and departments initiated by academic feminist activists in various universities (Kandiyoti, 2019; Arat, 2021) and a women's library and documentation centre (Kadın Eserleri Kütüphanesi ve Bilgi Merkezi Vakfı) as an association in 1990. These initiatives were instrumental in increasing the number of studies on women's issues, raising awareness, and institutionalising the women's movement (Diner & Toktaş, 2010).

Wither away "gender equality"; instead, go for "gender justice"

Until 2011, including the first term of the AKP, there had been legal and institutional improvements regarding gender equality. This was likely due to NGOs' active contestation and cooperation with the state that influenced the agenda of the policymakers. For example, the new labour law (4857) drafted in 2003 safeguarded gender equality in the workplace, although it had a neoliberal stance. The law legalised flexible work, part-time work, temporary and contract labour, and subcontracting (Ercan & Oğuz, 2014; Akçay, 2018), which empowered the employer and drastically changed working conditions. However, it also provided some provisions (such as job security after childbirth and protection from workplace harassment) that led to the betterment of the workplace for women employees (Ün, 2019; Karan, 2021). These provisions, especially those related to extended maternity leave and the obligation to provide childcare in the workplace for women employees, instigated a situation where employers started to employ fewer women. Thus, the participation of women in the labour market was limited to part-time or temporary jobs (Arat, 2021).

During this period, the responses of the government to NGOs and their campaigns was shaped with amendments to regulations and related legislation. The government and its agencies intended to control and coordinate women's issues centrally in a top-down fashion (Şenyücel, 2020). In line with the neoliberal populist patriarchal policies pursued by the AKP, the existing welfare regime was revised, and some social assistance devices like *Conditional Cash Transfers* (CCTs) and *General Health Insurance* were initiated. The goal of these devices was to secure the inclusion of informal workers to the social security system. For example, as discussed in Chapter 3, CCTs aimed to support lower income households without social security coverage for the education and healthcare of their children (Bergman & Tafolar, 2014; Şener, 2016; Karan, 2021). With the new welfare system – *General Health Insurance*- all sorts of health benefits were provided to those were not insured through a social security system. However, these devices which were intended to empower women turned out to be devices for distancing women from the labour market and repositioning them at home, at the service of the family members as a caregiver. (Şener, 2016). Furthermore, the direct relationship between the AKP cadres and the Directorate responsible for its implementation has been evaluated as the instrumentalisation of women voters for the elections (Akçay, 2018).

The Turkish government publicised its aim in diffusing gender equality, and in 2012 ratified the Council of Europe Convention on Preventing and Combating Violence Against Women and Domestic Violence, the *İstanbul Convention*. However, the same political party signed the withdrawal from the Convention in March 2021. The decision was made by the President and announced in the Official Gazette. The decision was criticised by women's and LGBTQIA+ organisations, opposition parties, bar associations, human rights organisations, various trade and labour unions, universities, and corporations. Protests continue to be organised by women's organisations all over the country, and groups of non-state actors applied to the Council of State to overrule the decision. The government still has not responded to this backlash.

In a similar vein, after the 2012 WEF meeting, country-level Gender Parity Task Forces were launched, which identified Turkey as one of the most problematic countries. Shortly after the meeting, the Equality at Work Platform was founded in Turkey under the Ministry of Family and Social Policies and with the co-presidency of Turkey's two leading holding companies (Sabancı and Doğuş). The Platform acted to safeguard gender equality for women in the labour market with an aim of minimising the gender gap in the economic realm. It was expected that the Platform would promote gender diversity. In so doing, the host of the Platform, that is, the Ministry of Family and Social Policies, organised meetings for business leaders and human resources workgroups and informative workshops for NGOs and academicians. They even prepared a booklet for best practices and videos for "The role model woman employee" (Vargeloğlu, 2020). Participation in this platform was voluntary. However, many companies preferred to comply only with legal requirements rather than being part of such an initiative. Companies that were involved in the Platform made announcements that they were committed to gender equality at work as a social responsibility or sustainability project. On the other hand, state authorities were hesitant to amend the necessary legal framework to support diversity initiatives such as setting quota systems for women employees for the overall labour force as well as for the managerial positions. Currently, neither companies nor the related government agencies provide information about the Platform. Was it a "window dressing" performance staged by the state agencies in cooperation with the corporations (Özsoy et al., 2019)?

Given all these changes and the steps taken for maintaining gender equality in society and in the workplace, the discourse started to change after 2011. One of the indicators of this shift was noted in a speech by Prime Minister Erdoğan at a meeting where he declared that he did not believe in equality of men and women. The attendees were members of non-state women organisations who had been working with state offices and representing Turkey in the international arena on gender issues (Kandiyoti, 2019). In 2011, the prime minister announced that the Ministry of Women and Family Affairs would be replaced with the Ministry of Family and Social Policies that would organise the General Directorate of the Status of Women, the General Directorate of Family and Social Services, and Services for Disabled and the Elderly under one roof. The termination of the Ministry of Women and Family Affairs was a violation of international agreements such as CEDAW and conflicted with the constitution (Arat, 2021). This was an institutional change that deliberately eliminated gender equality and relegated women to positions as family members and caregivers. The justification for such a move was provided by Prime Minister Erdoğan: "We are a conservative democratic party. The family is important to us" (Belge, 2011). So, women and equality began to disappear from governmental discourse. Non-state actors and women's organisations were not silent. They voiced their concerns and organised a campaign in which more than 3,000 signatures were collected and presented to the prime minister, but nothing has changed.

Another development during this period that shaped this move was the emergence of new actors in the women's movement: The pro-government conservative women's organisations such as the Women and Democracy Organisation (KADEM), the Women's Rights Organisation against Discrimination (AK-DER), and the Women Health Workers Association for Solidarity (KASAD-D) (Ün, 2019). In an effort to marginalise the oppositional women's organisations comprised of left-oriented, secular, professional women, the AKP supported these new actors in creating a public sphere where gender equality norms were disrupted and replaced by gender justice. Gender justice advocates the claim that the "sameness" emphasis of gender equality leads to a situation where women are masculinised and lose their feminine differences. These new organisations are not independent of the state; on the contrary, they are deliberately positioned by the state as a countervailing power for the existing non-state women's organisations. Ün (2019) explicates this situation with the following example.

> In 2014, the Ministry of Family and Social Policy announced that KADEM, AKDER, KASAD-D were the three NGOs who would send representatives to a committee that would designate Turkey's nominees for GREVIO-an independent body of experts which monitor the implementation of the Istanbul Convention; independent women's organisations were excluded from the GREVIO (Group of Experts on Action against Violence against Women and Domestic Violence – İstanbul Convention) candidate selection process.
>
> (p. 42)

From 2011, the neoliberal, populist policies pursued by the AKP and the authoritarian, conservative tone widened the gender gap and, furthermore, spread inequalities. The government, by either neglecting or by subverting gender equality norms (Ün, 2019), developed a milieu where "gender equality" is contested and women are relegated to their homes as caregivers. In addition, the existing institutions which prioritised women were replaced with those which bring family to the centre. So, these groups see women's roles as centred around the family. Furthermore, the empowerment of pro-government women's organisations that promote "gender justice" led to the marginalisation of non-state actors supporting "gender equality". Driven away from the decision-making process of the governmental offices, gender equality supporters positioned themselves as the overseers of actions taken by the state.

Gender diversity?

Given these background conditions, we can say that currently women in Turkey are distanced from the labour market, must deal with the discriminatory practices of their employers, and have less and less presence as owners, managers, and board members. According to the 2021 Global Gender Gap Report, Turkey is ranked 133rd out of 156 countries. The change in gender gap from 2010 to 2021 can be seen in Table 3.1.

Table 3.1 Widening gender gap (2010–2021)

	2010 rank	*2010 score*	*2021 rank*	*2021 score*
Global Gender Gap Index	126	0.588	133	0.638
Economic participation and opportunity	131	0.386	140	0.486
Educational attainment	109	0.912	101	0.975
Health and mortality	61	0.976	105	0.967
Political empowerment	99	0.077	114	0.123
Labour force participation rate	n.a.	0.35	137	0.494
Wage equality for similar work	n.a.	0.398	95	0.617
Legislators, senior managers, and officials	n.a.	0.110	133	0.193
Professional and technical workers	n.a.	0.540	117	0.567

Source: World Economic Forum (2010), Global Gender Gap Report 2021 and 2010

Women in economic participation, educational attainment, health and mortality, and political empowerment are in a disadvantageous position. The situation is more accentuated in the labour market; more women are employed as part-time workers as compared to men. They also experience a "motherhood pay gap" (i.e., mothers earn less than women without children) of 30 percent (ILO, 2019), and during maternity leave, they are paid only 66.7 percent of their annual gross wage. Furthermore, women's presence in the top management echelons (as a professional manager or as a member of the board of directors) is minimal (see Table 3.2). Finally, according to a study conducted by the International Labor Organization (ILO) Turkey and Turkish Statistical Institute, the gender wage gap is 15.6 percent. The gap widens as the age increases and as the education level decreases (ILO, 2020).

The reasons behind this dark picture can also be explained by the actions of the companies and the state. It is not only that governmental authorities are indecisive in implementing diversity programs but also that companies are reluctant to engage voluntarily in such practices. Unless there is a reward, companies seem to reason that it would not be a viable move to start gender diversity initiatives of any type. Especially in the presence of neoliberal policies and pervasive managerialism, any strategy other than one based on financial gains would be difficult to incorporate into the corporate agenda. As mentioned above, the partnering companies of the Equality at Work Platform positioned their involvement as a social responsibility or

Table 3.2 Gender gap indicators in the labour market, 2021

	Female	*Male*
Unemployed adults, percent of labour force	16.73	12.60
Workers employed part-time, percent of labour force	32.56	18.67
Boards of listed companies, percent board members	18.10	81.90
Firms with female majority ownership, percent of firms	11.30	88.70
Firms with female top managers, percent of firms	3.90	96.10
Length of maternity/paternity leave, (days) weeks	16	1
Wages paid during maternity/ paternity leave, percent annual gross wage	66.70	100.00

Source: World Economic Forum (2021), Global Gender Gap Report (2021)

sustainability initiative while circumventing their legal responsibilities for gender equality. The following report on the "dismissal of a female employee for requesting her employer to provide childcare" prepared by Bakırcı, (2019) for the European Commission, European Equality Law Network explicates the position taken by the companies.

> According to Labour Law (4857) ratified in 2003 and regulations drafted in 2013, it is the responsibility of the employer to provide nursing rooms (if the company employs 100–150 women workers) and childcare centres (if more than 150 women are employed) in the workplace. The case reported is related to a bank which employs more than 1000 women and does not have a childcare centre. One of the women employees, who was on leave for family related matters, via an official letter asked the bank authorities to establish a childcare centre. The letter also stated that the absence of a childcare centre might cause her to be terminated in line with the Labour Law. What were the consequences of this demand for a childcare centre which was a legal requirement?
>
> The bank did not establish the childcare centre. Did not allow the female employee to return to the workplace and regarded her warning as a resignation.
>
> The issue was carried to the labour court. The decision of the court was in favour of the employer.

> The women employee filed an appeal to the higher court.
> The higher court decided that the employer terminated the employment contract without just cause and therefore the applicant should receive severance and notice pay.

As can be seen from this report and many other similar examples, the companies prefer to defer their legal responsibilities. Law enforcement is weak, even negligible. So, the establishment and services of childcare centres and nursing rooms are easily avoided. Accordingly, in an effort to bypass their legal obligations, companies have started to employ fewer women.

Conclusion

Gender diversity practices in Turkey are aligned with the policies adopted by the state towards women, and they are shaped by the power relationships between the state and the non-state actors. From the early years of the Republic, the state policies shaping women's inclusion in the public sphere have been identified as securing women's rights to participate in politics, education, and labour markets, and these rights were secured by drafting related legislation. In this "state sponsored feminism" (Kandiyoti, 1991) period, the relationships between state and non-state actors advocating women's rights were sidelined by the government cadres in a process of co-optation. The role assumed by non-state women's organisations was confined to philanthropy. In the post-1980 period, there has been a proliferation of non-state organisations claiming gender equality that were founded and run by left-oriented, professional groups. These organisations, through contestation and cooperation, forced state agencies to build institutions and draft legislation for gender equality. In 1986, CEDAW was ratified, and in the early 2000s, changes in criminal and civil codes were made. In a similar vein, institutions such as the Directorate on the Status and Problems of Women and later a ministry for women and family, research centres in universities, and documentation centres for women studies were established.

A drastic move from this period of equality, participation, and presence in the public and economic realm came after 2011. The government and the ruling party through deliberate neglect and replacement of the existing institutions for gender equality have marginalised the women's movement and reduced the status of women to be caregivers. Furthermore, the labour laws designed in line with neoliberal policies that empower the employer turned out to be an instrument for displacing women from the labour market and full-time employment. In this transformative process, oppositional women's organisations were distanced from the local decision-making process, representation in international organisations (for example, the UN Commission on the Status of Women), and replaced by pro-government women's organisations that opted for gender justice based on Islamic principles. These organisations render domestic violence as a gender-neutral issue, do not question patriarchy, and reconstruct women's identities in relation to the family as mothers, caregivers, and supportive wives (Ün, 2019). In such a milieu, gender diversity is subverted to a corporate social responsibility issue rather than a right. It became a game started by international organisations, the state, and publicly listed companies where the participants (the state agencies and companies) believed that such engagement could lead to access to powerful positions. As the state moved away from gender equality, the engagement of listed companies in gender diversity has become limited to their public relations efforts that aim to enhance their status vis-à-vis their rivals and building public visibility.

References

Akçay, Ü. (2018). *Neoliberal Populism in Turkey and Its Crisis*. IPE Working Papers 100/2018, Berlin School of Economics and Law, Institute for International Political Economy (IPE). Retrieved from https://ideas.repec.org/p/zbw/ipewps/1002018.html

Arat, Y. (2021). Democratic backsliding and the instrumentalization of women's rights in Turkey. *Politics & Gender*, 1–31. https://doi.org/10.1017/S1743923X21000192

Bakırcı, K. (2019). *European Network of Legal Experts in Gender Equality and Non-Discrimination, European Commission*. Retrieved from www.equalitylaw.eu/downloads/4943-Turkey-the-dismissal-of-a-female-employee-for-requesting-her-employer-to-provide-childcare-pdf-90-kb

Belge, B. (2011, June 9). *Women Policies Erased from Political Agenda*. Bianet. Retrieved from https://bianet.org/bianet/women/130607-women-policies-erased-from-political-agenda

Bergmann, C., & Tafolar, M. (2014) *Combating Social Inequalities in Turkey Through Conditional Cash Transfers (CCT)*? (Conference Proceeding), 9th Global Labor University Conference "Inequality within and among Nations: Causes, Effects, and Responses". Berlin School of Economics and Law.

Diner, C., & Toktaş, Ş. (2010). Waves of feminism in Turkey: Kemalist, Islamist and Kurdish women's movements in an era of globalization. *Journal of Balkan and Near Eastern Studies*, 12(1), 41–57. https://doi.org/10.1080/19448950903507388

Ecevit, Y. (2007). Women's rights, women's organizations and the State. In Kabasakal, A. Z. (Ed.), *Human Rights in Turkey* (pp. 187–201). University of Pennsylvania Press.

Ercan, F., & Oğuz, Ş. (2014). Rethinking anti-neoliberal strategies Through the perspective of value theory: Insights from the Turkish case. *Science and Society Quarterly*, 71(2). https://doi.org/10.1521/siso.2007.71.2.173

ILO. (2019). *A Quantum Leap for Gender Equality: For a Better Future of Work for All*. International Labour Office. Retrieved from www.ilo.org/global/publications/books/WCMS_674831/lang-en/index.htm

ILO. (2020). *Measuring the Gender Wage Gap: Case of Turkey, ILO Turkey Office and TurkStat*. Retrieved from www.ilo.org/ankara/publications/WCMS_756660/lang-en/index.htm

Kandiyoti, D. (1991). End of empire: Islam, nationalism and women in Turkey. In *Women, Islam and the State* (pp. 22–47). Palgrave Macmillan.

Kandiyoti, D. (2019). Against all odds: The resilience and fragility of women's gender activism in Turkey. In Kandiyoti, D., Al-Ali, N., & Poots, S. K. (Eds.), *Gender, Governance and Islam*. Edinburg University Press.

Karan, U. (2021). *Country Report Non-Discrimination: Transposition and Implementation at National Level of Council Directives 2000/43 and 2000/78: Turkey 2021*. Publications Office of the European Union. https://doi.org/10.2838/373975

Özsoy, Z., Şenyücel, M., & Oba, B. (2019, July 4–6). *Gender Diversity Practices, in Search of Equality or Window Dressing*? [Paper Presentation]. 35th European Group for Organisational Studies Colloquium. Edinburgh.

Sancar, S. (2012). *Türk modernleşmesinin cinsiyeti: Erkekler devlet, kadınlar aile kurar* [The Gender of Turkish Modernization: Men Establish the State, Women Establish the Family]. İletişim Publishing.

Şener, M. Y. (2016). Conditional cash transfers in Turkey: A case to reflect on the AKP's approach to gender and social policy. *Research and Policy on Turkey*, 1(2), 164–178. https://doi.org/10.1080/23760818.2016.1201246.

Şenyücel. M. (2020). *The Dialectic Between Institutional Pluralism and Field Level Responses* [Unpublished Doctoral dissertation, Istanbul Bilgi University]. Istanbul Bilgi University Research Repository.

Tabak, H., Erdoğan, S., & Doğan, M. (2022). Fragmented local normative orders, unresolved localizations, and the contesting of gender equality norms in Turkey. *Asian Journal of Women's Studies*, 28(2), 143–166. https://doi.org/10.1080/12259276.2022.2059737

Ün, M. B. (2019). Contesting global gender equality norms: The case of Turkey. *Review of International Studies*, 45(5), 828–847. https://doi.org/10.1017/S026021051900024X

Vargeloğlu, A. C. (2020). *Toplumsal cinsiyet perspektifinden bütçeleme ve yerel yönetimlerde cinsiyete duyarlı bütçeleme yaklaşımı* [Budgeting from a Gender Perspective and a Gender-Sensitive Budgeting Approach in Local Governments] [Master's thesis, Muğla Sıtkı Koçman University]. Muğla Sıtkı Koçman University Research Repository.

World Economic Forum. (2010). *Global Gender Gap Report 2010*. Retrieved from www.weforum.org/reports/global-gender-gap-report-2010/

World Economic Forum. (2021). *Global Gender Gap Report 2021*. Retrieved from www.weforum.org/reports/global-gender-gap-report-2021

4 International organisations

Initiators and facilitators

Introduction

Gender diversity as a managerial practice is a fairly new phenomenon on the Turkish corporate landscape (Erdur, 2022). Initiation of a new practice takes some time during which existing mindsets, habits, and norms need to be transformed by the deliberate actions of informed actors (Pless & Maak, 2004, Santamaría et al., 2015). Like many other business initiatives in Turkey (Selekler-Goksen & Yildirim Öktem, 2009), gender diversity has been realized by the active involvement and guidance of international organisations that led projects for improving gender equality in Turkey.

With the exception of multinational enterprises operating in Turkey, Turkish companies – even the biggest ones – were not aware of the importance of diversity programs until the equality in the workplace initiative, which was introduced by the WEF and led by the Turkish government. After the 2012 WEF meeting, the equality in the workplace group was established under the leadership of the Ministry of Family and Social Policy and two big business groups (Sabancı and Doğuş). This was the most powerful initiative in Turkey up to that time, and we discuss its background story in the following section. The same year, the Equality in the Workplace Platform was established to improve Turkish women's position in society (WEF, 2016).

The WEF and the Gender Parity Task Forces

In 2012, the WEF mobilized task forces in three countries that had a high gender gap – Mexico, Turkey, and Japan – by launching action-oriented projects at the national level. In 2014, the Republic of Korea, where the gender disparity is also high, was added to the same study. The task forces formed in line with the premises of the project tried to create collaborations between the public and private sectors to accelerate participation of women in economic activity at all levels. The first step was to identify obstacles

DOI: 10.4324/9781003244868-5

to women's participation and advancement in the workforce. Afterwards, providing a neutral platform for dialogue, the task force proposed solutions for the specific conditions of each country. Aiming to improve relations with the EU and other international platforms, the Turkish government was more strongly involved in Davos that year, and they undertook that mission diligently. Thus, what the Turkish government did at that time was to push Turkish companies to implement gender diversity practices in their organisations. Generally, the aim of this initiative was to understand the barriers to women's economic participation and advancement. WEF stated that country task forces in Mexico, Japan, Turkey, and Korea attempted to enable interaction between businesses and state institutions in employment-related issues such as recruitment, retention and career advancement, pay parity, workplace culture, national policies and regulations on parental leave, and encouraging women entrepreneurship (WEF, 2016).

The Turkey Gender Parity Task Force was established in 2012 by the Ministry of Family and Social Policies and the heads of the two big holding companies in Turkey. Under the benefaction of the WEF, gender diversity practices were mainly initiated by Fatma Şahin, then the minister of Family and Social Policies in the third cabinet of AKP between 2011 and 2013. In 2012, the minister got together with the most prominent Turkish business leaders and their teams, and they gathered around a very large U-shaped table. The minister gave a well-prepared presentation about the project called "equality in the workplace". One of the participants in the project explained her observations about the meeting:

> I think her goals are extremely high, what do I know about the key performance indicators, road map reporting, the measurement was a beautifully organized presentation with everything. It did not seem like everyone was admiring the subject and that these guys were not just faking it out with some shallow rhetoric. They made a beautiful presentation.

After that presentation, the minister announced that they had decided to start with the biggest companies in Turkey. She asked who wanted to participate in the project – which was a rhetorical question – and all the attendees raised their hands.

> It wasn't possible to say that I wouldn't, so all the major actors in the Turkish business world that were called into that hall that day actually became a stakeholder" said the same witnesses of that day.

About 80 of the largest employers in the country became members of the Equality at Work Platform. The Platform mainly featured members from the financial services industry (17 percent), the mobility industry (11 percent), the consumer industry (12 percent), and cross-industry conglomerates (12 percent). The task force, which included many civil society leaders, established a multi-stakeholder structure, analysed "economic gender equality", and put forward the "Equality at Work Declaration" containing 11 principles. Practices took place in the task force's first 18 months on issues such as leadership training for women, monitoring systems to determine gender differences in hiring ratios, and incorporating gender data into proposals when drafting supplier contracts.

The key performance indicators were already determined by the system, and companies were expected to enter the quarterly data through a special portal. The ministry followed up on that and reminded companies if they entered the data late. After Fatma Şahin left office, the project was over. Moreover, after 2013, the government of Turkey also lost its focus on maintaining continued good relationships with international organisations, including the EU. This project lasted only one and a half years; it is a dead project right now. The portal and the website are no longer available. However, the project initiated momentum for gender diversity within Turkish business circles.

The WEF report titled "Equality in the Workplace" gives examples of best practices in many companies on gender equality. For example, by tracking the employment and recruitment rates of women at all levels in a specific company affiliated with a holding, which is among the leaders of the task force, it is stated that the rate of female recruitment increased from 21 percent to 40 percent between 2012 and 2014 (WEF, 2016). However, we have to indicate that, in this specific case, the company operates in the service sector where women work intensively. Thus, it is an exceptional case, and the vast majority of publicly traded companies avoid giving figures about the increase in the female employee ratio. For example, another task force leader, a holding company, developed a mentoring program for female employees in 2014 to further women's career development and to eliminate the gender gap between managers and senior managers. When the web pages and activity and social responsibility reports of the two large publicly traded companies chairing the task force are examined, it can be seen that the development is very limited, especially in the male-dominated sectors. Moreover, although there were many positive examples in the report prepared by the task force at the end of the third year, it is seen that the examples were limited to either single cases (for example, they covered only certain companies and not all holding companies) or their quantitative evaluations were not very clear.

The WEPs: good at committing, bad at executing

The history of women's studies in Turkey is also related to the UN Women's Conference held in Mexico City in 1975. As in many countries, the issue of women in development (WID) entered the global agenda at this first international meeting and led to the formation of a brand-new administrative and intellectual system (Kandiyoti, 2010). Thus, we can say that UN has also played a crucial role in the women's agenda.

In 2014, a much more common initiative came into the itinerary of big Turkish companies. The Women's Empowerment Principles (WEPs) were a joint initiative of UN Women and the Global Compact that was launched on International Women's Day in March 2010. The WEPs are designed as a managerial guide especially for the business world. The WEPs are a tool designed for the private sector's work on gender equality, and they are based on seven principles[1]. By signing the WEPs, companies that deal with a wide range of issues – including women's senior corporate leadership, the prevention of discrimination, and the development of opportunities such as training and courses for women on social initiatives and advocacy – promise to implement these principles (Gürer et al., 2017). Therefore, the WEPs intend to provide not only guidance for the business world, but also a control mechanism and an opportunity for self-assessment for companies.

In May 2014, under the leadership of the UN Global Compact Turkey, the Women's Empowerment Working Group was established to be open to the participation of representatives from the private sector, civil society, academia, government agencies, and UN institutions. The group provides a platform that supports the sharing of good practices on women's empowerment. In 2017, the UN Global Compact, together with private sector and civil society, published the WEPs Implementation Guide (2017) that aims to guide private sector institutions in their work on women's empowerment in their workplaces and areas of activity. The guide, which contains detailed information about the principles, presents the steps that companies can take to implement the principles after they sign the CEO Support Statement, in which they state their intention to implement the WEPs. In addition to providing new participants with ways to implement the principles to which they are committed, the guide also includes examples of companies that will inspire more active ways to participate. This was the latest activity of the Global Compact in Turkey for the promotion of the WEPs principles.

The WEPs have been signed by 6,793 companies worldwide as of 30 July 2022. There are 437 business participants from Turkey, making Turkey one of the leading signatory countries in terms of the number of companies that have signed these principles. More specifically, Turkey ranks second after

Brazil, which has 660 signatories. China follows Turkey in third place with 333 signatory companies (www.weps.org/companies).

UN Women Turkey organizes many activities with the private sector within the framework of the WEPs in Turkey. For example, in 2021, cooperation was made with TÜSİAD to develop the "Gender Sensitive Crisis Management Guide" with a focus group study that allows companies operating in different sectors to share their experience (UN Women Turkey, 2022). However, the WEPs are not legally binding but soft law principles to be applied contingently to the specific conditions of those who declared their commitment to following them. Moreover, on the WEP's website, 36 companies are listed in "the Countries of the WEPs implementation" category and there is no company from Turkey on this list. Though Turkey is one of the champions in terms of signing the principles and declaring commitment through their websites and various platforms, Turkish companies are not active in execution.

Other private sector partnerships of UN women Turkey: equality blah blah blah

UN Women states its engagement with private sector companies within the scope of global programs implemented to achieve gender equality at the national level. Other than the WEPs for gender equality and women's empowerment in business and social life, UN Women Turkey leads initiatives such as the UNSTEREOTYPE Alliance to eliminate stereotypes in marketing and communication and HeForShe to ensure men's solidarity with women and break harmful stereotypes.

HeForShe is defined as a global movement that calls on men to be in solidarity with women and advocates of gender equality in Turkey's largest private sector organisations. One of the biggest conglomerates in Turkey was among the 36 global leaders of the HeForShe movement run by the UN Women. The communication director of an holding company that we interviewed considers the movement to be a communication activity:

> "HeForShe" was exactly what we wanted. Because we had already started to do great things in terms of content, but the awareness side, that is, the most attractive part was still missing. "HeForShe" completed just that. There are no key performance indicators or anything binding in the content of "HeForShe", it is an awareness campaign in its entirety. It's just a slogan, actually. Gender equality is not a women's problem; it is a common problem for all humanity. Because this is a human rights issue. In fact, we can solve this problem when men, the

> other 50 percent of humanity, embrace this job and work with women. Of course, the role models they use from Obama to Matt Damon are celebrities and popular people from the world of politics and sports. We were our president at that time. We became its spokesperson in Turkey.

At the HeForShe Summit in May 2020, a five-year period was evaluated and the "Guide to Gender Equality in Communication" developed by the holding company was selected among the "Good Practices". The "Guide to Gender Equality in Communication" is a tool that uses a gender filter, the language used in advertisements and communication and offers a methodology to transform the language (Günay et al., 2022, March 20). Within the scope of the same project, Gender Equality Workshops are held. More than 100 marketing professionals, including marketing department representatives from group companies as well as communication experts and more than 30 advertising, PR, and social media agencies, participated in the workshops.

Using gender-inclusive language guidelines to promote gender equality through language, the UNSTEREOTYPE Alliance is a platform for ideas and action to transform harmful gender stereotypes in media outlets and advertisements. Founded by UN Women, the UNSTEREOTYPE Alliance consists of global members and allies, leveraging the global influence of the UN as well as national chapters that take a global approach to local, culturally driven stereotypes – applying a global vision to local goals. As of 2021, the platform had 11 national chapters and 217 global members around the world, including the Turkey Section. Sixteen companies from Turkey are members of the platform.

Another initiative of UN Women Turkey involves generation equality. The Generation Equality Forum is a global multi-stakeholder initiative for gender equality co-hosted by the Mexican and French governments and coordinated by the UN Women's Unit (UN Women, 2022). The Forum was held in Mexico in March and in Paris in June 2021. In line with the vision set out in the Generation Equality Forum and the Beijing Declaration and Plan of Action, UN Women aims to accelerate gender equality gains before 2030. The Forum will continue for five year 'action journey' based on a series of concrete, predictive, and transformative actions, including a financial assessment of $40 billion (Generation Equality Forum, 2022)

"Being among one of the global leaders of the Technology and Innovation Action Group, which is also one of the six action coalitions as part of the generation equality forum, a big Turkish listed firm undertook another task in the efforts to ensure gender equality on a global scale for five years with the HeForShe Project.

As has been discussed so far, there are the various projects led by UN Women in collaboration with the Turkish business community including big firms as well as business-initiated NGOs. Most of the projects do not have the capacity to transform existing practices within the firms. Instead, these projects aim to raise awareness within the business community or help disadvantaged women to enhance their capacity using different tools. Action Coalitions is a good example of such projects, and it calls diverse stakeholders to come together for "commitments, resources and action" (UNSTEREOTYPE Alliance, 2022). Thus, this kind of initiative is warmly welcomed by the Turkish business community as there is no need for solid execution or results.

Joint projects of listed companies and ILO: workshops, commitments, training

Turkey has signed ILO conventions 100, 111, 122, and 142, which ensure equality between men and women and promote women's employment. The ILO runs the Reputable Business Country Program in many countries around the world. In this context, Turkey signed the Memorandum of Understanding on the National Respectable Work Programme on 10 February 2009, in Lisbon, where the 8th European Region Meeting of the ILO was held. In so doing, the government of Turkey and the ILO declared that they would implement the National Decent Work Program with the cooperation of social partners in Turkey. Accordingly, the issues of ensuring gender equality and increasing women's employment were determined to be among the articles they agreed to. With the signed National Decent Work Program, the importance of promoting decent work for women and increasing women's employment was emphasized once again.

In this framework, in light of the general policy of the ILO on the development of women's employment and the low female employment rate in Turkey, the ILO Ankara Office in cooperation with the Turkish Employment Agency (İŞKUR) established the Active Labour Market Policies Pilot Project for Realizing Gender Equality through the Provision of Decent Work Opportunities, with the aim of improving women's employment in Turkey in 2009.

The joint report titled "Global Overview of Working Conditions" published by the ILO and the European Research Organization (Eurofound) in May 2019 provided a striking comparative analysis of job quality worldwide, including in Turkey, in terms of working hours, gender pay gaps, and skills development opportunities. According to the report, one-third of workers in the EU experience intensive work (very short deadlines and high-speed work); half of the workers in Turkey are faced with intensive work. Working hours vary widely among countries; while one-sixth of the workers in EU countries work more than 48 hours a week, almost half of the workers in Turkey do this. While more than 70 percent of workers in the Republic of Korea can take an hour or two off to deal with their personal or family situation, this figure is 20 to 40 percent in Turkey, according to the report. Regardless of country, people with the lowest levels of education have less access to opportunities to grow and develop skills. While the rate of people who state that they learned new things while working varies between 72 percent and 84 percent in the EU, the rate in Turkey is 57 percent (Eurofound et al., 2019). Considering the high rates of female employment in the informal sector in Turkey, it can be concluded that the ILO's definition of decent work is far from conforming to the four basic structures, namely, standards and fundamental rights in working life, social dialogue, social security for all, and productive employment.

Another project of ILO Turkey was the More and Better Jobs for Women: Women's Empowerment in Turkey through Decent Work project. Phase I was funded by the Swedish International Development Cooperation Agency (SIDA) between 2013 and 2018, with the support of the ILO and the İŞKUR. The first phase of the project was intended to ensure women's access to decent work opportunities and raise awareness about gender equality and working conditions to support the strengthening of women's employment in Turkey. Phase II, called the More and Better Jobs for Women Program, was financed by SIDA and implemented within the scope of the Gender Equality at Work Portfolio of the ILO Office for Turkey. Within the scope of the program, various projects were carried out in six different provinces to encourage women's access to employment opportunities and to improve women's working conditions in collaboration with İŞKUR, the General Directorate of Labour and other relevant public institutions, workers' and employers' organisations, as well as the private sector.

Four targets were set in the ILO project: Gender-based wage gap, gender-based violence at work, work-life balance, and women's leadership. Two objectives were determined within the scope of the project: 1) creating more and better job opportunities for women seeking employment in Turkey and 2) promoting decent working conditions for women in working life. İŞKUR, employers' organisations, universities, and the Ministry of Family, Labour and Social Services were among the project partners of the ILO.

In order to ensure gender equality in working life and to prevent gender-based wage inequality, the ILO Turkey Office, which prepared a joint report with the Turkish Statistical Institute (TUİK) on the calculation of the gender pay gap, this time started to work on measuring the gender pay gap at the company level (ILO, 2021). In the report of the ILO Turkey Office and TURKSTAT, the gender pay gap in the public sector in Turkey was 5.1 percent, while this rate was calculated as 15.3 percent in the private sector. The solution offered by the organisation in solving the problem was awareness, education, guidance, and information transfer. The ILO declared that the training program could be a guide for companies as well as a tool to raise awareness on the subject. The program included interactive applications and exercises through which the participants pointed out the reasons behind the inability to fully measure the gender-based wage gap in institutions due to numerous variables.

Consequently, the main project stakeholders of ILO Turkey are government offices, trade unions, NGOs, and universities. On the business side, they mention some ILO-supported pilot projects with small and mid-size companies. When it comes to big companies, including listed firms, there are only a few endeavours, most of which seem to be more PR-work-oriented. It seems that, by various research endeavours, the ILO addresses problems that hinder women's labour force participation, retainment, and advancement. But when it comes to solving the problem, the subject is shifted to another medium. When we look at the projects that Turkish companies have developed together with the ILO to solve the problems, it is seen that what has been done does not go beyond the "soft methods" that the business world favours, such as making commitments, raising awareness, and providing training.

Violence and harassment in the workplace are among the biggest barriers to women's access to work, their retention, and promotion to higher positions. Offering an inclusive and gender-sensitive approach, ILO Convention No. 190 was proposed as a fundamental step in combating violence against women (ILO, 2021). For the first time, in an international convention that was adopted in 2019 on the 100th anniversary of the founding of ILO, the convention defined violence and harassment in the world of work as a violation of human rights and a threat to equal opportunities. Turkey is not among the countries that have ratified this convention. So, ILO Turkey endeavours to encourage and keep the issue on the agenda by various activities such as publishing the Women at Work Violence and Harassment Combat Handbook (ILO, 2022) and organizing meetings, workshops, and press releases with the participation of different stakeholders.

World Business Council for Sustainable Development

The Sustainable Development and Business World Association, which was founded as Turkey's arm of the World Business Council for Sustainable Development (WBCSD), also established a working group in the field of gender diversity. After the sustainability development goals were announced, one of the four focus areas which were determined as a result of the workshops that were held with the members and stakeholders of the association was "social inclusion". Under this focus area, in 2016, the Working Group on Women's Employment and Equal Opportunities was established.

Thus, as the representatives of the Turkish business world, they chose to emphasise productivity and efficiency from a utilitarian perspective. This working group was established under the chairmanship of one of the leading Turkish holding companies with the aim of "raising awareness, developing strategies and collaborations to create workplaces sensitive to gender equality and increasing the number of companies working and reporting on gender equality in the business world". Research carried out in the field of gender equality in the business world included a case study that would be inspired by companies that had not yet started working on this issue by bringing together good practices. In order to realize this idea, the projects of companies that are members of the association and also signatories of the WEPs were selected within the scope of the funding provided by a Turkish bank (TSKB) and the French Development Agency (AFD). Thus, what they did was mostly a corporate communication activity. Soon this initiative established a platform called Eşit Adımlar (Equal Steps) (SkdTurkiye, n.d.) to publicise the "best practices" of Turkish firms. When the declarations of this platform are analysed, most of the "gender friendly" initiatives of the companies can be considered as either social responsibility projects that aim to "help" women and young girls to gain new skills through various programs both within and outside the firm or as projects to raise awareness for a more egalitarian society in terms of gender equality.

Conclusion

In this chapter, the findings regarding projects that have been realised by the active involvement and guidance of international organisations such as the Women's Empowerment Principles and HeForShe are discussed. These projects are involved in improving gender equality in Turkey. Furthermore, relationships among various international organisations and national organisations are discussed in order to aid the debate on how these relationships might have facilitated or obstructed field activities. The major questions tackled in this chapter are related to the capacity of these projects to change the status quo.

Although there is social pressure created by various international initiatives such as the UN WEPs and HeforShe, the results of the projects do not have transformative capacity. UN Women's collaborations with private sector companies are on a voluntary basis and confined mainly to publicity, awareness raising, and communications. Thus, international organisations emerge as the most important actors in the initiation of diversity programs in the business world. However, these organisations do not have the authority to put pressure on the business world unless they are supported by the state.

International organisations have the power to create change only when they have the support of the Turkish governments.

As the practice of equality in the workplace shows us, an initiative headed by the WEF can mobilise the business world with the support of the state. However, the same project ended after one-and-a-half years when the state withdrew its support. Many large companies involved in the project continue to implement diversity programs. However, to a large extent, these programs do not go beyond public relations activities. Moreover, the major achievement of the Platform, which operated as a project of the Ministry of Family and Social Policies, was publishing pamphlets and booklets and shooting videos on role model women employees.

In Turkey, the issue of gender diversity is embodied by the interactions of three power centres: the business world, the state, and international organisations. The global "institutionalisation" of standards and practices regarding gender equality in the economic field materialises through the United Nations (UN Women) and major international organisations. We can say that international organisations, especially UN Women, play a leading role in bringing the issue of gender diversity to the agenda in the Turkish business world and in determining the standards. However, the view that the development-based approaches of the UN deepen rather than reduce the gender gap is common among feminist groups (Kandiyotti, 2010).

The initiation and funding of projects on gender equality by international organisations is known as the NGOisation of feminism and the rise of "project feminism" (Diner & Toktaş, 2010) This issue is being studied on a global scale and has been criticised by feminist groups. We can say that the programs carried out under the leadership of international organisations contribute to the empowerment of women. We observed an increase in the number of initiatives operating to improve women's rights and status in the business world through projects. However, due to the nature of the business world, its approach to women's issues is pragmatic and not rights based. Therefore, even if those who carry out these projects are women, their class priorities take precedence over women's identities. In other words, the staff actively working in gender diversity in NGOs and initiatives supported by or established by international organisations are often representatives of the business world. Naturally, these organisations are not always managed by people who are sensitive to women's equality, but by people who serve the profit maximisation purpose.

Diner and Toktaş (2010) drew attention to the fact that representatives of some transnational companies participate in UN conferences under the guise of NGOs, advocating business or industry. Similarly, UN Women chose Turkey's largest holding company as its partner. Since 2011, the

AKP government's move away from the West has reduced the prestige of international organisations in the eyes of the state. Therefore, the power of these institutions to exert pressure on the state, enforce policies to protect women's rights, and combat discrimination against women is very limited. Having said that, unless supported by the state, the activities of international organisations cannot go beyond researching and publishing, raising awareness, forming public opinion, and sponsoring advocacy activities. For example, the ILO's Ratifications of C190 – Violence and Harassment Convention has not been approved by the Turkish government. In the studies of both international organisations and academic researchers, violence and harassment are two of the most important issues that women may encounter in their participation in business life, and both affect their chances of promotion. However, it is not possible to prevent violence and harassment against women in the workplace unless there are legal sanctions, and the necessary mechanisms are established within companies. Without the necessary legal arrangements, what international organisations such as the ILO can do is limited to bringing the issue to the agenda and sharing information and experience.

Notes

1. Establish high-level corporate leadership for gender equality
2. Treat all women and men fairly at work – respect and support human rights and non-discrimination
3. Ensure the health, safety, and well-being of all women and men workers
4. Promote education, training, and professional development for women
5. Implement enterprise development, supply chain, and marketing practices that empower women
6. Promote equality through community initiatives and advocacy
7. Measure and publicly report on progress to achieve gender equality

References

Diner, C., & Toktaş, Ş. (2010). Waves of feminism in Turkey: Kemalist, Islamist and Kurdish women's movements in an era of globalization. *Journal of Balkan and Near Eastern Studies*, 12(1), 41–57. https://doi.org/10.1080/19448950903507388

Erdur, D. A. (2022). Diversity and equality in Turkey: An institutional perspective. In *Research Handbook on New Frontiers of Equality and Diversity at Work.* Edward Elgar Publishing.

Eurofound, Aleksynska, M., Berg, J., Foden, D., et al., (2019). Working conditions in a global perspective. *International Labour Organisation.* https://data.europa.eu/doi/10.2806/870542

Günay, M., İnan, M., & Yılmaz, Ç. (2022, March 20). *Kahramanlar zirvede buluştu.* Milliyet. Retrieved from www.milliyet.com.tr/gundem/kahramanlar-zirvede-bulustu-6722097

Gürer,P., Özman, B. O.; & Çamdereli R. (2017). Women's empowerment principles (weps) implementation guide: Equality means business. *UN Women.* Retrieved from https://eca.unwomen.org/sites/default/files/Field%20Office%20ECA/Attachments/Publications/2017/WEPs_Implementation%20Guide_EN.pdf

ILO (2021). *Çalışma yaşamında şiddet ve taciz: 190 sayılı sözleşme ve 206 sayılı tavsiye kararına ilişkin rehber* [Violence and Harassment at Work: Guidance on Convention 190 and Recommendation 206]. Retrieved from www.ilo.org/wcmsp5/groups/public/-europe/-ro-geneva/-ilo-ankara/documents/publication/wcms_840841.pdf

ILO. (2022). *Çalışma yaşamında kadınlara yönelik şiddet ve tacizle mücadele el kitabı* [Handbook on Combating Violence and Harassment Against Women at Work]. Retrieved from www.ilo.org/wcmsp5/groups/public/-europe/-ro-geneva/-ilo-ankara/documents/publication/wcms_731371.pdf

Kandiyoti, D. (2010). Gender and women's studies in Turkey: A moment for reflection? *New Perspectives on Turkey*, 43, 165–176. https://doi.org/10.1017/S089663460000580X

Pless, N., & Maak, T. (2004). Building an inclusive diversity culture: Principles, processes and practice. *Journal of Business Ethics*, 54(2), 129–147. https://doi.org/10.1007/s10551-004-9465-8

Santamaría, L., & Santamaría, A. (Eds.). (2015). *Culturally Responsive Leadership in Higher Education: Promoting Access, Equity, and Improvement* (1st ed.). Routledge. https://doi.org/10.4324/9781315720777

Selekler-Goksen, N. N., & Yildirim Öktem, Ö. (2009). Countervailing institutional forces: Corporate Governance in Turkish family business groups. *Journal of Management & Governance*, 13(3), 193–213. https://doi.org/10.1007/s10997-009-9083-z

SkdTurkey. (n.d.). *About Us*. Retrieved from www.skdturkiye.org/esit-adimlar/hakkimizda

Unstereotype Alliance. (2022, August 18). *Annual Report 2021*. Retrieved from www.unstereotypealliance.org/en/resources/research-and-tools/2021-annual-report

UN Women. (2017). *Kadının güçlenmesi prensipleri (weps) uygulama rehberi* [Women's Empowerment Principles (weps) Application Guide]. Retrieved from www.globalcompactturkiye.org/wp-content/uploads/2019/01/WEPs_Rehber.pdf

UN Women (2022). *Highlights from 2021: UN Women in Turkey*. UN Women. Ankara. Retrieved from https://eca.unwomen.org/sites/default/files/2022-04/Highlights%20of%202021.pdf

World Economic Forum. (2016). *Closing the Economic Gender Gap: Learning from the Gender Parity Task Forces*.

5 Non-governmental organisations

Advocates

Introduction

Business associations have been viewed as key organisations in the dissemination of neoliberal politics in economic, social, cultural, and political realms. However, there are also many other characteristics of civil society organisations in Turkey with different ideologies, which have been supported by the Turkish government to advance such causes. Turkish legislation classifies NGOs as trade associations, unions, employers' organisations/professional federations, NGOs, service and production associations, local government associations, political interest groups, religious interest groups, and others (Ministry of Development, 2018; Talas, 2011). Recent reports suggest that the Independent Industrialists and Businessmen Association (MÜSİAD), an industrialists' and businessmen's association known for carrying an Islamic identity, has become the main NGO that gains support from the government diffusing "justice rhetoric" – a shifted gender equality statement which we will mention shortly – in the workplace (MÜSİAD, 2021a, 2021b, 2021c, 2021d, 2022a, 2022b, 2022c). TÜSİAD is also another business association that has a more secular orientation, but it has also been supported by the big capital, boss organisations. Through various mechanisms, TÜSİAD motivates member companies to include gender issues in their policymaking agenda. Thus, we call these organisations the supported actors of gender diversity and inclusion.

Furthermore, besides business associations, there are women's organisations such as the Women's Labour and Employment Initiative Platform (KEIG), the Women Labour Platform (KEP), the Women's Solidarity Foundation (KADAV), the Women's Support Association (KA.DER), and various other NGOs that are oppositional to or do not emphasise Islamist and governmental activities. These organisations promote gender diversity and inclusion programs with a feminist or left-wing ideology. However, especially after 2011 with a shift from gender equality to gender justice in the

DOI: 10.4324/9781003244868-6

discourse adopted and practices developed by government officials, these feminist and pro-gender equality organisations have been marginalised. They are excluded by the government from the decision-making process in women's issues and representing Turkey in international organisations. Instead, newly established pro-government NGOs, mainly supporting gender justice, are included in the decision-making process and have taken their position in the international organisations for handling gender issues in Turkey.

The supported actors of gender diversity and inclusion

In order to advance EU accession negotiations, Turkey actively worked to fulfil Copenhagen political criteria (Saatçioğlu, 2009). Its success in earlier negotiations initiated a governmental agenda towards strengthening civil society organisations and developing human rights protection and promotion communities (Duman, 2017). Within negotiations collaborations between government offices, non-governmental and international organisations have been encouraged to mobilise publicly listed companies towards implementing diversity and inclusion programs (McKinsey & Company & TÜSİAD, 2017). This meant that NGOs achieved a powerful position in the Turkish business environment to shape the gender equality agenda until 2011.

International organisations have been the dynamo that diffused "gender equality" discourse within Turkish NGOs with an emphasis on benefits such as increased economic growth, corporate performance, and employee health (McKinsey & Company & TÜSİAD, 2017). In line with the vigorous environment generated by international organisations, local NGO campaigns have been heavily dependent on their funding. In the early 2000s, Turkish NGOs received most of their funding from organisations such as the UN, the WB, and the EU which influenced their agenda and policymaking process (Kardam, 2004; Kandiyoti, 2019). This process reflected neoliberal economic and social priorities and resulted in the "de-politicisation of feminist demands" (Kandiyoti, 2019, p. 88).

After 2011, the agendas of most international organisations shifted to immigrant and refugee issues, and organisations stopped funding local NGOs that were focused on gender issues. In line with these changes, the state phased out its collaborative work with NGOs. Instead, the state authorities turned NGOs' power loss into an opportunity to become a self-sustaining entity. This means that the government has been developing its own agencies and pro-government organisations and maintaining relations with big capital to sustain its power against oppositional NGOs and women's organisations. Accordingly, the gender equality agenda was transferred to organisations such as Human Rights and Equality Institution of Turkey (called the Turkish Human Rights Institution at that time), Borsa Istanbul,

Capital Markets Board of Turkey, or the Turkish Ministry of Family and Social Services. For example, the promotion and monitoring of participation in economic decisions has been implemented by Capital Markets Board since 2012 (Sancar, 2018, p. 153).

This process accelerated and paved the way for temporary work arrangements within private employment offices as well as the regulation of women's roles in society for flexible work with lower wages (Aras, 2013; Mülkiye Haber, 2015). Accordingly, legal requirements have been shaped towards equal treatment; maternity, paternity, and breastfeeding leave; and short-term and part-time work within Labour Law 4857, State Officials Law 657, Public Servants' Unions Law 4688, Trade Unions and Collective Labour Agreement Law 6356, Occupational Health and Safety Law 6331, Social Insurance and General Health Insurance Law 5510, Unemployment Insurance Law 4447 (ÇSGB, 2017). Most of the related articles were added or amended between the years 2003 and 2011.

In so doing, the government also supported the development of "gender justice" discourse and the practices of women's NGOs. With the inclusion of pro-government, pro-Islamist women's NGOs to the decision-making process (such as representation at the international organisations), oppositional pro-gender-equality NGOs were marginalised even more and dragged down from the policy advancements on gender diversity.

In its rhetoric, MÜSİAD currently expresses justice with statements of oppression:

> "(Çerçeve (Frame) Magazine . . . continued to be the voice of oppressed geographies and . . . brotherly societies" (MÜSİAD, 2022b). "With the thought that Turkey should continue to be a shelter for the oppressed, MÜSİAD studies focused on social cohesion projects and humanitarian diplomacy activities, especially with the contribution of young and female businesspeople" (MÜSİAD, 2022a). "MÜSİAD's priority is the Islamic world. MÜSİAD's priority is the oppressed nations" (MÜSİAD, 2022c). "Women who wear headscarves are denied entry to university, their right to work is deprived, they suffered a violation of rights that is unprecedented in the history of the world." (MÜSİAD, 2022b)

In addition to statements emphasising entrepreneurship, oppositional NGOs argue that entrepreneurship is being used to cover the increase in informal employment of women, and they also release statements about sustainability, reflecting the modern business world: "We are taking decisive steps in guiding our women entrepreneurs regarding development agencies, KOSGEB (Small and Medium Enterprises Development Organisation of Turkey), relevant ministries and EU projects" (MÜSİAD, 2021a).

At MÜSİAD's latest general assembly, only two female members were appointed to the board of directors, one of whom is a substitute member (MÜSİAD, 2022c). One female member is also the head of MÜSİAD's women's committee, and she recently stated:

> As we are the businesswomen's community, we believe that increasing the number of female employers in the business world, developing and strengthening this potential will undoubtedly contribute positively to both employment and the economy of the country. Women's workforce participation is also very important for the sustainability of economic and social life. We say "sustainability" because the development and dissemination of practices that maintain the balance of work and private life will bring about an increase in productivity and motivation. At the same time, digital entrepreneurship plays an important role in contributing both economic growth, employment opportunities and innovation. As women in business life, one of our important areas of work is to support women's entrepreneurship and to strengthen existing initiatives. In this sense, we are aware of our responsibility in providing training and mentoring infrastructure to entrepreneurial activities, facilitating access to the network and acting as a bridge.
>
> (MÜSİAD, 2022a, p. 52)

However, it seems that MÜSİAD became involved in gender-related practices only recently. The foundation of its organisational activities relies on Islamic ideology. For instance, the book written about their 25-year history by Dönmez (2015) notes that their members are motivated by the divine right and justice to advance every activity they participate in. Gender equality and inclusion are out topics, where not even the word "women" is used in the book.

> All around the world, with Islamic sensitivity, rights, people who have internalised the concept of justice, have that idea that he must fight, and that he should not be waiting any results from it. Because it's a long road.
>
> (Dönmez, 2015, p. 83)

Nevertheless, it is not only Islamic or pro-government organisations, but also big capital that has been influenced by the state's rhetorical shift. For instance, TÜSİAD has been a major actor in the implementation of gender diversity practices. The organisation has been preparing equality-focused reports since 2000 (TÜSİAD, 2000; TÜSİAD & KAGİDER, 2007), and its political campaigns have started lobbying for companies to provide nursery services for female employees. In the early 2000s, provision of nursery services was considered a governmental responsibility, so TÜSİAD became an advocate to convince governmental agencies to act. Then TÜSİAD and major sector associations (for example, the Advertisers Association, Advertising Foundation, Association of Communications Consulting Companies, Public Relations Association of Turkey, and Association of Corporate Communicators) prepared a campaign with the slogan "Gender roles have already changed; why not change what we watch on TV?" They also extended this activity to television series (İnceoğlu & Akçalı, 2018). Furthermore, in a recent report, the organisation issued a call for all political parties, opinion leaders, the academic community, and non-governmental and media organisations to bring about a new mindset to the business environment. They discussed workplace inclusion-related issues within themes related to human development and competence, science, technology and innovation, and political, economic, and social institutions and rules. In these themes, the commonalities towards female labour participation are that Turkey would be a fairer place to work when more women are appointed to technology-driven and institutional jobs.

> What we aim to achieve . . . is a fair Turkey that provides equitable income, eliminates regional disparities, ensures gender equality, where everyone lives equally and freely without discrimination as to language, religion, sect, race, and origin, and does not leave any segment of society behind during the development process.
>
> (TÜSİAD, 2021)

Indeed, their call aroused heated arguments in the Turkish media. For example, Adıgüzel and Uzuntel (2021) responded with the financial difficulties university students in metropolitan cities face. They mentioned working conditions where female students could mostly find daily jobs for hourly wages. Various other issues such as the lack of governmental support, lower wages in comparison with male counterparts, as well as changing attitudes of house owners towards female students needing to rent, and the problems in girls' dormitories were discussed (Adıgüzel & Uzuntel, 2021). Moreover, Oyan (2021) highlighted the relational changes between TÜSİAD and the government. The report argued that the Islamic power has been weakened, and TÜSİAD positioned itself according to the increasing public backlash against the existing government and the possible change of ruling party in the 2023 elections. Thus, it is claimed that TÜSİAD has been using the campaign as an instrument for competitive advantage, as a showdown with other capital groups. This position taken by TÜSİAD is explained by Sabuncu (2022) with a focus on a recent protest at a large retailer:

> TÜSİAD's "Build the Future" report, shows a stance that does the opposite of what it says. . . . So, who is the most talked-about businessperson in Turkey these days? (One of TÜSİAD's top executives). Why? Because, in a large retailer X, which he owns, the warehouse workers' current protest, about wages of 4 TL per hour and an increase for a bread price, were responded to by 257 workers layoffs. The Warehouse, Port, Shipyard and Marine Workers' Union (DGD-SEN) organised democratic and peaceful actions across Turkey so that nobody is left unaware of this injustice.

Women's organisations and other NGOs: the marginalised

In Turkey, women's organisations and platforms are homogeneous in terms of organisational responses, but they differ in terms of their focus on women's employment issues. Women lawyers, under the umbrella of the Turkish Bar Association, organised a workshop in 1999 titled "Equality of Men and Women in the Path to Democratisation and Disruptions in Practice". The main purpose of the event was to open a debate on how women's rights commissions could become pressure groups so that contradictory articles from the civil code could be annulled. With the guidance of this workshop, the Turkish Bar Association Women Rights Commissions Network (TUBAKKOM) was formed (Moroğlu, 2000).

Furthermore, KEİG was established as a response to the Women's Employment Summit of 2006. Members of the platform asserted that the summit excluded the experiences and demands of feminists as well as women's organisations. The organisation has an activist side for influencing public policies on women's labour, as well as an academic side focused on knowledge production. Accordingly, the platform conducts research on women's labour issues and prepares reports. For example, in its first report on women's employment and political suggestions, KEİG elaborated on important issues such as sexual discrimination, inequality in wages, and male dominance in unions (KEİG, 2009). In one of our interviews with a member of KEİG, it is stated that:

> KEİG was founded to be the intervener in the government's involvement in developing strong women's rights and women's employment opportunities, a process similar to EU accession. Till 2015, we were even invited to public meetings of the Ministry of Family and İŞKUR

> (Turkish Employment Agency). But we were criticising government policies at the same time. When the omnibus laws started to come out the government changed its attitude towards us. After 2015 the Swedish Development Agency also cut its funding, which made most of our branches impotent.

This situation is reflected in the decrease in the number of reports they shared after 2015. Nevertheless, in their latest report, KEİG focused on the economic crisis and its impact on women's labour (KEİG, 2019). Their report revealed that the Turkish women's labour force is still concentrated in low-skilled and informal jobs within an economy based on flexible work, which increases the risks of economic crises. The organisation directed attention to the need for empirical data on contraction and layoffs in sectors as a means of mobilising unions, as well as the lack of data on inflation rates and the purchasing power of families, where the only income earner is women, as a means of putting forward demands to social services in particular and social policymakers in general. The report also presented the idea that governmental agencies tend to pass their social responsibilities, such as child and elderly care services, on to women's cooperatives.

In their latest article, they discussed the worsening work conditions for service sector workers that were caused by the pandemic. They highlighted the increased working hours, inadequacies in access to protective equipment, inadequate disinfection and isolation in workplaces, lack of shuttle services for commuting, lack of breastfeeding breaks or not being able to take leave during menstruation days (Bilir & KEFA, n.d.). However, to prevent gender inequalities during the pandemic, KEİG also made several suggestions regarding the economic measures package of the government. The package included taking gender impact and evaluation measures for fiscal and monetary policies, obtaining opinions and support from those who work for gender equality in crisis management, ensuring compatibility between income tax regulations with progressive (fair) taxation system, reducing the VAT on basic necessities such as food, clothing, and cleaning and directing the infrastructure expenditures of this period to social infrastructure expenditures such as health and child and elderly care, where the effects of growth, poverty, employment, and gender equality are more pronounced, and implementing gender-sensitive budgeting in central and local governments (Yücel & KEFA, n.d.).

There are voluntary women's organisations and platforms such as KEP which were organised when the Turkish government publicised drafts of the omnibus law which included women's employment. KEP asserted that such legislation imprisons women in their homes (KEP, 2013). Another group, KADAV, includes 32 separate women's organisations from 16 different provinces, and its recent work focuses on violence and discrimination against Turkish women and immigrant women. KADAV offers design and production workshops for women where they can develop their sewing skills to a level that enables them to work in the textile field. The workshops also guide their careers and enable them to establish relationships with institutions where they can receive vocational training or business establishment support (KADAV, n.d.). In addition, the KADER (n.d.) organisation states that it was founded to eliminate gender inequality, with the aim of bringing women's experiences and abilities to social and political fields. The organisation, which publishes Turkey's social gender equality scorecard every 8 March, International Women's Day, stated in the latest report that the country received only a passing grade with regard to the number of women academic staff and headmen (KADER, 2022). However, these NGOs are outside the gender diversity initiatives of the Turkish business circles. In our interviews, business executives never mentioned these organisations as their stakeholders in implementing diversity practices. On the other hand, members of these platforms are not aware of the attempts taken by companies in relation to gender diversity.

There are also initiatives that specifically aim to promote gender diversity on the boards of directors among Turkish companies. The Independent Women Directors (IWD) project of Sabancı University Corporate Governance Forum in collaboration with Egon Zehnder International-Turkey is one of them (Ararat et al., 2018). They declare the mission of the initiative is promoting gender diversity on boards of directors and increasing the supply of female managers in Turkey. Though nine reports were compared, the number of female board members in Turkish-listed companies did not show a dramatic increase. Furthermore, in their current report on the data of 420 listed companies, the number of male managers is observed as five times higher than women (Sabanci, n.d.). However, it is also evident that the number of independent women directors has been increasing since 2012.

Another initiative promoting gender diversity on boards of directors is the mentorship program of Women on Board Turkey (WoB Turkey). They aim to connect talented female candidates with experienced businesspeople who are influential in appointing managers. As a recent signatory of the UN Global Compact, the organisation reported activities such as appointing women to boards of directors; increasing awareness about gender equality among women, leaders, and institutions for boards of directors; supporting the appointment of their graduates to boards of directors; nurturing the economic and political climate for more women on boards of directors; and creating the financial resources for sustainable operations (YKKD, 2021). The

Professional Women's Network Turkish Chapter is another not-for-profit global professional network that works for balanced leadership by building gender-balanced leadership programs. Finally, Women Corporate Directors Turkey offers training programs for potential women directors. They also organise events to raise awareness and to advocate quotas for women board members. Founded under the leadership of 13 private sector entities, the Business Council for Sustainable Development Turkey (BCSD) is another business association that develops projects on gender equality. The BCSD Women Employment and Gender Equality Working Group is involved in awareness-raising activities about social inclusion, developing and implementing strategies, and establishing cooperation for gender equality, as well as goal setting and systematic reporting related to women's employment and gender equality (BCSD Turkey, 2017).

NGOs that emphasise human resource development also struggle to mobilise diversity and inclusion in the workplace. PERYÖN, the earliest NGO founded to bring together human resources managers, academicians, and consultants on people management issues, initiated several projects to maintain gender equality on the agenda of the Turkish business environment. One of the representatives of the organisation explained this situation as such:

> We first tried to understand our situation with a survey. We applied to all companies we could reach regarding gender equality in business life in Turkey. And then, in 2012, we were asked to make a commitment to the most important pillar of this Equality at Work platform (there are more details about the platform in our listed companies' chapter). We came together for seven to eight months and prepared a very serious manifesto for the representatives of the institutions working on this issue and the ministry representatives. Every member prepared a series of commitments.

PERYÖN also initiated a project within the scope of the Hrant Dink Foundation Civil Society Development Grant Program and with the support of the EU. The project is called İş'te BirlİKte (In Work TogetHeR), and its purpose is to arrange human resources processes in a way that does not lead to discrimination concerning gender equality and sexual orientation, as well as to increase awareness about these issues among the decision makers and relevant actors (PERYÖN, n.d.). Within the scope of the project, meetings with companies from various cities, most of them being signatories of EU's WEP project, were organised. The notes of these meetings reveal the human resources practices adopted by the participant companies. Most of these practices are related to training and mentoring programs for women. They offer services in sectors that are characterised by a gender gap, introducing social responsibility projects concerning the strengthening of women's positions and maintaining social gender equality, and drafting policies for the prevention of violence against women (PERYÖN, 2020). The meeting report also stated that only a few multinational companies have an agenda on and comprehensive work for LGBTQIA+ individuals, as well as parental leave and supplier and dealer network participation (PERYÖN, 2020). The report also mentioned barriers such as the difficulty in attracting female candidates to sectors and positions seen as masculine, the discrimination between men's and women's work, the sociocultural structure of the society, prejudices towards women's participation in the labour market, self-limitation by women, and the effect of heavy housework responsibilities on female labour participation (Demirel, 2020).

The representatives at the meeting also mentioned how the pandemic affected gender diversity initiatives within their companies.

> During the pandemic the priority became the protection of human health and how we will manage this process. . . . Schools closed, workplaces locked down. . . . So, we decided to give an award for creating value in difficult times. In other words, diversity, employer brand lost its importance. But it also shows . . . what a weak bond we all have with diversity. We consider diversity as a project. It has not been a part of our daily life. For the first time, during the pandemic no company applied in the diversity management award category.

Conclusion

For three decades, NGOs have been the most significant advocates for gender diversity and inclusion in workplaces in Turkey. However, during the same period, the scale and scope of gender diversity activity changed in line with the shifts in power positions taken and discourses adopted by state officials and international organisations. These shifts promoted the establishment of new NGOs and shaped collaboration patterns between governmental and international organisations in promoting gender diversity practices. Prior to 2011, gender diversity practices were shaped with gender-equality discourse and the vision of mainly feminist and left-wing-oriented NGOs. These organisations developed projects funded by international organisations and collaborated with state agencies to draft legislation to protect women's rights in the workplaces. However, after 2011, with the deliberate policy of the ruling party, "gender equality" discourse and practices were replaced by "gender justice" discourse where men and women were taken as different in terms of their capacities and capabilities. The change in discourse was followed by the emergence of a new type of NGO that supports the government's new approach to women's issues. The government maintained strong relationships with pro-Islam and secular big capital organisations such as MÜSİAD and TÜSİAD. This conservative environment motivated governmental rhetoric shifts from gender equality to gender justice. These relationships also resulted in law amendments and the announcements of omnibus laws that brought flexible short-term jobs and lower wages as well as social roles that supported such labour. While these newly emerging NGOs moved to the centre and collaborated with the government in the decision-making and policy-drafting process, the former groups of NGOs that advocated gender diversity and inclusion were marginalised from the decision-making process and were driven to take an oppositional position. Oppositional NGOs lost their collaborative position with the state agencies and faced international funding cuts. This led to the dissemination of gender justice discourse among business environments.

References

Adıgüzel, H., & Uzuntel, S. (2021, November 2). *TÜSİAD'ın raporu ve geleceği inşa meselesi* [TUSİAD's Report and the Issue of Building the Future]. Retrieved April 4, 2022, from www.evrensel.net/haber/446771/TUSİADin-raporu-ve-gelecegi-insa-meselesi

Ararat, M., Alkan S., & Aytekin, B. (2018). *5th Annual Report Women on Board Turkey*. Retrieved from https://kadinliderlikplatformu.org/paylasimlarimiz/women-on-board-turkey-5th-annual-report-iwd-project/

Aras, Z. (2013). *AKP'nin "Kadın İstihdam Paketi"* [AKP's "Women Employment Package"]. *Marksist Tutum*. Retrieved from https://marksist.net/zehra-aras/akpnin-kadin-istihdam-paketi.htm

Bilir, Z. E., & KEFA. (n.d.). *Covid 19 salgınının hizmet sektöründeki kadın istihdamına etkileri*. [Effects of the Covid 19 Epidemic on Female Employment in the Service Sector]. Retrieved from www.keig.org/covid-19-salgininin-hizmet-sektorundeki-kadin-istihdamina-etkileri/#_ftn1

BCSD Turkey. (2017). *Women Employment and Gender Equality*. Retrieved from www.skdturkiye.org/en/kadin-istihdami-ve-firsat-esitligi

ÇSGB. (2017). *Çalışma hayatında kadın* [Women in Working Life]. Retrieved May 5, 2022, from www.csgb.gov.tr/media/1319/calismahayatindakadin_bilgilendirme-rehberi.pdf

Demirel, A. P. (2020). *Yuvarlak masa toplantıları özeti* [Roundtable Meeting Summary]. Retrieved May 5, 2022, from www.istebirlikte.org/wp-content/uploads/2020/12/Yuvarlak-Masa-Toplantilari-Ozeti.pdf

Dönmez, A. (2015). *25 Yılın hikayesi* [The Story of 25 Years]. MÜSİAD. Retrieved May 5, 2022, from www.MUSİAD.org.tr/uploads/yayinlar/ozel-yayinlar/pdf/25-yilin-hikayesi.pdf

Duman, E. (2017). *Prohibition of Discrimination and People in Turkey: Rights and Equality Institution Report*. Ayrıntı Publishing.

İnceoğlu, İ., & Akçalı, E. (2018). *Social Gender Equality at Television Series Research*. Retrieved May 5, 2022, from https://TUSİAD.org/tr/yayinlar/raporlar/item/9943-televizyon-dizilerinde-toplumsal-cinsiyet-esitligi-arastirmasi

KADAV (n.d.). *Tasarım ve üretim atölyeleri* [Design and Production Workshops]. Retrieved May 5, 2022, from https://kadav.org.tr/calismalarimiz/kadin-emegi-ve-istihdami/tasarim-ve-uretim-atolyeleri/

KADER (2022). *Geleneksel 8 Mart karnesi* [Traditional March 8 Scorecard]. Retrieved May 5, 2022, from http://ka-der.org.tr/8-mart-karnesi/

KADER (n.d.). *Hakkımızda* [About Us]. Retrieved May 5, 2022, from http://ka-der.org.tr/hakkimizda/

Kandiyoti, D. (2019). Against all odds: The resilience and fragility of women's gender activism in Turkey. In Kandiyoti, D., Al-Ali, N., & Poots, S. K. (Eds.), *Gender, Governance and Islam*. Edinburg University Press.

KEİG. (2009, April). *Türkiye'de kadın emeği ve istihdamı sorun alanları ve politika önerileri* [Women's Labour and Employment Issues in Turkey and Policy Recommendations]. İstanbul. Retrieved May 5, 2022, from www.keig.org/wp-content/uploads/2016/03/keig-platformu-politika-raporu_2009.pdf

KEİG. (2019). *Kriz, kadınlar ve kadın emeği forumu raporu* [Crisis, Women and Women's Labour Forum Report]. Retrieved May 5, 2022, from www.keig.org/wp-content/uploads/2019/01/Kriz-Kadinlar-Kadin-Emegi-Forumu-Raporu.pdf

KEP. (2013, November). *Kadın istihdam tasarısı kime müjde* [Women Employment Scheme, Good News for Who]. Istanbul. Retrieved from http://docplayer.biz.tr/3374147-Kadin-istihdami-yasa-tasarisi-kime-mujde.html

McKinsey & Company, & TÜSİAD. (2017). *Women Matter Turkey 2016 Turkey's Potential for the Future: Women in Business*. Retrieved July 14, 2022, from https://TUSİAD.org/en/reports/item/9642-women-matter-Turkey-2016-report-Turkey-s-potential-for-the-future-women-in-business

Ministry of Development. (2018). *Kalkınma sürecinde sivil toplum kuruluşları özel ihtisas komisyonu raporu* [Civil Society in the Development Process Organizations Special Commission Report]. Ankara.

Moroğlu, N. (2000). *Yasalarda kadın erkek eşitliğinin sağlanması ve uygulamada karşılaşılan aksaklıkların giderilmesi için kadın avukatların iş birliği* [Cooperation of Women Lawyers for Ensuring Equality in Law and Elimination of Problems Encountered in Practice]. İstanbul.

Mülkiye Haber. (2015). *Özel istihdam büroları kadınlar için çözüm mü?* [Are Private Employment Agencies the Solution for Women?]. *Mülkiye Haber.* Retrieved from https://mulkiyehaber.net/ozel-istihdam-burolari-kadinlar-icin-cozum-mu/

MÜSİAD. (2021a, November–December). *Çerçeve Dergisi* [Frame Magazine]. Retrieved July 14, 2022, from www.MUSİAD.org.tr/uploads/press-349/cerceve_98sayi_web.pdf

MÜSİAD. (2021b). *Çerçeve Dergisi* [Frame Magazine]. Retrieved July 14, 2022, from www.MUSİAD.org.tr/uploads/press-349/cerceve_97sayi_web.pdf

MÜSİAD. (2021c). *Çerçeve Dergisi* [Frame Magazine]. Retrieved July 14, 2022, from www.MUSİAD.org.tr/uploads/press-349/cerceve_96sayi_web.pdf

MÜSİAD. (2021d). *Çerçeve Dergisi* [Frame Magazine]. Retrieved July 14, 2022, from www.MUSİAD.org.tr/uploads/press-349/cerceve_95sayi_web.pdf

MÜSİAD. (2022a, May–June). *Çerçeve Dergisi* [Frame Magazine]. Retrieved July 14, 2022, from www.MUSİAD.org.tr/uploads/press-364/cerceve-dergisi-sayi-101-web.pdf

MÜSİAD. (2022b, Mar–April). *Çerçeve Dergisi* [Frame Magazine]. Retrieved July 14, 2022, from www.MUSİAD.org.tr/uploads/press-354/cerceve_100sayi_web.pdf

MÜSİAD. (2022c, January–February). *Çerçeve Dergisi* [Frame Magazine]. Retrieved July 14, 2022, from www.MUSİAD.org.tr/uploads/press-349/cerceve_99sayi_web.pdf

Oyan, O. (2021). *Patronların raporu: Türkiye'nin değil 'TÜSİAD'ın geleceğinin inşası'* [The Bosses' Report: 'Building the Future of TUSİAD, Not Turkey']. Retrieved April 4, 2022, from https://haber.sol.org.tr/haber/gorus-patronlarin-raporu-turkiyenin-degil-TUSİADin-geleceginin-insasi-316509

PERYÖN. (2020). *İş yerlerinde çeşitliliği destekleme projesi yuvarlak masa toplantıları* [Supporting Diversity in the Workplaces Project Roundtable Meetings]. Retrieved April 6, 2022, from www.istebirlikte.org/wp-content/uploads/2020/12/Yuvarlak-Masa-Toplantilari-Ozeti.pdf

PERYÖN. (n.d.). *Çalışma hayatının çeşitlilik odaklı yapılandırılması* [Diversity-Focused Structuring of Working Life]. Retrieved April 6, 2022, from www.iste-birlikte.org/proje-hakkinda/

Saatçioğlu, B. (2009). How closely does the European Union's membership conditionality reflect the Copenhagen criteria? Insights from Turkey. *Turkish Studies*, 10(4), 559–576. http://doi.org/10.1080/14683840903384802

Sabancı University. (n.d.). *9th Annual Report Women on Board 2021 Turkey*. Retrieved May 5, 2022, from www.yonetimkurulundakadin.org/assets/node_modules/source/pdf/sabanci-2021-9th_annual_report.pdf

Sabuncu, M. (2022, February 21). *TÜSİAD'ın 'geleceği inşasını, yüksek istişare konseyi başkanı çöpe attı* [TUSİAD's 'Building the Future' was Thrown away by the Chairman of the High Advisory Council]. Retrieved April 4, 2022, from https://t24.com.tr/yazarlar/murat-sabuncu/TUSİAD-in-gelecegi-insasi-ni-yuksek-istisare-konseyi-baskani-cope-atti,34301

Sancar, S. (2018). *Siyasal kararlara katılımda toplumsal cinsiyet eşitliği: Haritalama ve izleme çalışması* [Gender Equality in Participation in Political Decisions: Mapping and Monitoring Study]. CEID. Retrieved from www.ceidizleme.org/medya/dosya/94.pdf

Talas, M. (2011). Sivil toplum kuruluşları ve Türkiye perspektifi. *Türklük Bilimi Araştırmaları*, 29, 387–401. Retrieved from https://dergipark.org.tr/en/pub/tubar/issue/16970/177312

TÜSİAD. (2000). Kadın-erkek eşitliğine doğru yürüyüş: Eğitim, çalışma yaşamı ve siyaset [The Walk Towards Gender Equality: Education, Work Life and Politics]. Retrieved May 5, 2022, from https://TUSİAD.org/tr/yayinlar/raporlar/item/1866-kadin-erkek-esitligine-dogru-yuruyus-egitim-calisma-yasami-ve-siyaset

TUSİAD. (2021). *Building the Future with a New Mindset: People, Science, Institutions*. Retrieved May 5, 2022, from https://TUSİAD.org/en/reports/item/10864-building-the-future-with-a-new-mindset-executive-summary

TÜSİAD & KAGİDER. (2007). *Türkiye'de Toplumsal Cinsiyet Eşitsizliği: Sorunlar, Öncelikler ve Çözüm Önerileri* [Gender Inequality in Turkey: Problems, Priorities and Solutions]. Retrieved May 5, 2022, from https://TUSİAD.org/tr/yayinlar/raporlar/item/1944-turkiyede-toplumsal-cinsiyet-esitsizligi-sorunlar-oncelikler-ve-cozum-onerileri

YKKD. (2021). *YKKD Etki raporu* [WOB Turkey Impact Report]. Retrieved May 5, 2022, from www.womenonboardTurkey.org/assets/uploads/ykkd_impact_report_2020-2021.pdf

Yücel, Y., & KEFA. (n.d.). *COVID 19 salgını ve Türkiye'nin maliye politikaları* [COVID 19 Outbreak and Turkey's Fiscal Policies]. KEİG. Retrieved from www.keig.org/wp-content/uploads/2020/05/COVID-19-Salgper centC4per centB1n-per centC4per centB1-ve-Tper centC3per centBCrkiyeper centE2per cent80per cent99nin-Maliye-Politikalarper centC4per centB1.pdf

6 Trade unions

The alarming absence of women

Introduction

> The dispute continues within the Turkish Employers Association of Metal Industries (MESS) group contract negotiations, which concerns approximately 150 thousand workers in the metal industry. Over the past few days, various actions were held in factories where metal unions were organised. Union member women workers took the lead in actions such as marches inside the factory, press statements and not working overtime. . . . The workers, who stated that the union brought women to the forefront at the protests and tried to organise it especially, expressed their satisfaction with this on one hand, but also mentioned their discomfort at being held like a "Subject Model" on the other. . . . A young female worker said, "We are holding the flags in front rows, yes. We like this too. We are excited and eager. . . . However, the union is not with us in many problems experienced by women workers in the factory. This makes us doubt. The union is really trying to keep the actions alive. However, in the back of our minds, there is the possibility that this situation is insincere. . . . Another female worker criticised the fact that there is no voice about the "women's committees" that were announced to be included in the draft: "We are at the forefront of the protests, but there is no voice from the committee to be formed. The representatives say nothing".
>
> (Aksu, 2020)

> "MESS signed a miserable contract: Workers wanted 50 percent, unions said, "yes" to 27.44 percent" (Evrensel, 2021). "Thousands of Turkish Metal worker members came together at the rally in Kocaeli against MESS's imposition of a 17 percent misery interest, saying, "Our right to collective bargaining is our weapon to strike".
>
> (Ekmek ve Gül, 2022)

OECD and ILO rates for trade union membership densities demonstrate a decreasing trend for most countries in the last 20 years (ILO, 2022; OECD,

DOI: 10.4324/9781003244868-7

2022). It is evident that Turkish union membership rates have been below the average densities. Although ILO (2020) reported that female participation was higher than males in European countries, Turkish literature discusses the gender gap in Turkish union membership as well (Keleş, 2018; Urhan, 2017). It is argued that women are working predominantly as civil servants and as subcontracted personnel which makes it difficult for them to participate in trade unions (Keleş, 2018). Moreover, the lack of data about employment conditions, youth, and LGBTQIA+ in union membership complicates the identification of women's presence in unions from an intersectional lens (ETUC, 2021; KAOSGL, 2021). Another issue is the lack of information on how the recent Covid-19 pandemic affected female membership and managerial positions in trade unions. It can be argued that the unexpected changes in working conditions might have slowed down union activism and may have deepened inequalities in the labour market, for income, and for household responsibilities (Baycık et al., 2021; Bonacini et al., 2021; Gökçe, 2021; Meçik & Aytun, 2020; Yildirim & Eslen-Ziya, 2021). Given these constraints, it is vital not only to highlight women's alarming absence in trade unions, but also to seek how gender diversity practice is progressing in the Turkish context.

Turkish trade unions in retrospect

The attitude and practice of Turkish trade unions in relation to gender and diversity can be explained in relation to the tropes of neoliberal policies and divergence among extant trade unions in terms of their ideologies towards gender issues, that is, gender equality or gender justice.

One of the major changes in the Turkish labour regime was the adoption of a new labour law (4857) in 2003. The law was drafted in line with neoliberal policies – such as flexible work; part-time, temporary, and contract labour; and subcontracting (Ercan & Oğuz, 2015; Akçay, 2018) – and preceded the liberalisation of labour markets. The new legislation, while empowering the employers with various amendments (such as allocating weekly working hours, increasing daily work hours, and determining starting times and breaks), subordinated the workers (Özdemir & Yücesan-Özdemir, 2006). The new legislation, besides commodifying work, enfeebled unions and limited collective bargaining (Çelik, 2015; Akçay, 2018). Consequently, Turkey currently scores quite low on trade union membership (9.8 percent) and collective bargaining coverage rate (7.4 percent) according to ILO (2022a, 2022b) statistics. Furthermore, while the membership rates for left-wing unions decreased, the members of the pro-Islamist right-wing unions increased after 2002 (Çelik, 2015).

Among the left-wing Turkish trade unions, it is argued that the neoliberal order leads to de-unionisation and thus the exploitation of labour.

These arguments revolve around interventions on flexible labour and subcontracting arrangements that weaken employee bargaining power. As the state tends to abdicate not only from social services in particular, but its social, economic, and political responsibilities in general, firms restructure work and work-related gender norms to maintain their power position in the economic realm. Consequently, opportunities for forcing legislation in the interest of female and minority workers not only lessen, but employees also find difficulty in forming social dialogues with employers to develop gender-diverse practices in the workplace (Cam, 2019). Exclusion of the labour force from the decision-making processes and the pacification of their demands result in deteriorating working conditions, increasing levels of arbitrary layoffs, and unemployment (Çoban, 2013; TOKAD, 2011; Tokat & Aslan, 2009). Similar studies, in relation to Turkey and various other countries, discuss the role of neoliberal policies on the scope and scale of diversity management practices (for example, Özbilgin & Yalkın, 2019; Özbilgin & Slutskaya, 2017; Özbilgin, 2015). However, these studies rarely argue the influence of the neoliberal policies on the gender diversity practices of Turkish trade unions.

Currently, the Turkish labour regime embraces two conflicting types of union activism: the supporters of "gender justice" and the supporters of "gender equality" (Tabak & Doğan, 2022). The former group is characterised as pro-Islamist, pro-government (for example, HAK-İŞ), while the second group is considered to have a more left-wing orientation (for example, DİSK). Regardless of their political orientation, adherence to neoliberal norms and alliance with the state all the extant trade unions bring gender equality to their political agenda (Tabak & Doğan, 2022).

For instance, even though the state has formed committees to control collective bargaining practices to be in line with neoliberal policies, there has been continuous disagreement about wage levels and legislation among TURK-İŞ (the proponent of secular, Kemalist nationalism and defendant of the state's official approach to women's issues), DİSK, and the state (Önder, 2016, pp. 193–209). HAK-İŞ (pro-Islamist, conservative, and a right-wing union) members do not go on strike even if the union administrators seem to be in disagreement with the state. HAK-İŞ shares similar ideologies (i.e., gender justice rather than gender equality) with the Ruling Party towards women's emancipation (Arıcan, 2018; Birelma, 2021; Keleş, 2022). Furthermore, union reports and the academic literature show that left-wing unions (such as DİSK, KESK) are more inclined to defend social democracy (for example, see DİSK, 2022a, 2022b) while right-wing, pro-government unions (such as HAK-İŞ, Memur-Sen) favour the neoliberal, conservative, and populist ideologies of AKP (for example, Tabak & Doğan, 2021; Gök, 2021). Consequently, it can be argued that a right-wing union defending conservative roles of women would be unlikely to motivate the union members towards promoting women into managerial positions. Given this background on the liberalisation of the labour market, the empowerment of the employers, the enfeeblement of trade unions, and the diversity of existing unions in political orientation and approach to women issues, we can claim that diversity management in Turkey is an illusion. Right-wing, pro-Islamist unions, in line with the state cadres, support "gender justice" and neglect women and women's issues. Left-wing unions adopt a discourse for gender equality but in practice, they fall far behind in implementing this premise in their own organisation.

Women's union membership and unions having women managers in Turkey are influenced by the changes in the labour market profile, amendments in collective bargaining legislation, an increase in religious organising, diffusion of flexible work and subcontracting arrangements, internal dynamics of unions, as well as competition among the unions (Birelma, 2021; Çoban, 2013, Keleş, 2018). Thus, before we try to understand how motivated Turkish trade unions are towards workplace gender diversity, we anticipate that Turkish corporations would not be inclined to implement diversity practices. In previous chapters, we discussed policies assumed and initiatives taken by the state and the corporations on gender diversity. We expect that the unions would retain a marginal role in the implementation of these practices. Our observations led us to conclude that the state avoids diversity, and corporate practice is aligned only with legal requirements. Moreover, the lack of studies on gender diversity practices of the unions as well as the fact that Turkish unions are dominated by men (Birelma, 2021; Keleş, 2018; Kopuk & Taşoğulları, 2019; Urhan, 2017) also suggest that the unions would demonstrate less interest in a gendered workforce. In the top management cadres of the biggest unions, TÜRK-İŞ and HAK-İŞ, there are no women managers. The exception is at DİSK where the president is a woman. According to the Türer mapping study (2020), there are no women managers at the headquarters and branches of nearly all unions; there are slightly more women as workplace representatives. The data provided shows that women are excluded from the process. Unions employ women mainly for staff positions. The majority of the unions do not have an active commission for women's issues, although it is specified in their statues.

Ultimately, we found some support for the discussions mentioned above. Our analysis did not reveal interviewee discussions about neoliberal factors, as they have neither significantly mentioned the state as the actor that determines the dialogue between companies and unions, nor did they give significant examples of collaborative work towards diversity programs. Instead, they exhibited interest in dialogues about gender diversity competencies in improving the representation of women in Turkish trade unions. However, the majority of the interviewees also mentioned contextual barriers such as financial difficulties, lack of authorisation for collective bargaining, absence of professionalisation, or the lack of commitment to gender diversity practices. These obstacles seem to demotivate managers towards having dialogues with corporations for gender-sensitive practices. In short, our observations demonstrate that the strategies unions could formulate within their limited resources as well as the pressures from international organisations companies faced have shaped agreements towards workplace gender diversity. One of the consultants that works for a left-wing trade union summarised the process as such:

> On one hand, we do not have professional staff and on the other hand, employers do not want to get too much involved in these issues. If there is something that has been identified by the collective bargaining agreement, she/he tries to leave it on paper.

Discussions concerning Turkish unions also highlight the influence of an authoritarian regime on local power relations (for example, Berk & Gumuscu, 2016). Authoritarian regime changes are defined mainly as attempts in favour of developing conservative citizenship practices and national identities. In terms of work-based relations and rhetorical constraints of authoritative order, both challenge the democratic character of union relations and impede the transformation of business norms. The authoritative regime serves the preservation of conservative roles and traditional practices and eventually limits organisational commitment towards advancing women's employment rights and managerial status (Tokat & Aslan, 2009; Yılmaz, 2018; Yılmaz & Turner, 2019). In relation to the Turkish context and the repressive measures in the media and the judicial, military, and business fields involving politicised institutions, mass arrests and imprisonments, restricted strike rights and freedom of speech, and wide-scale censorship continue (Akyol, 2016; Human Rights Watch, 2014). In this environment, intolerance toward protests and strikes obstructs the maintenance of social dialogue, democratic representation, and social opposition for trade unions.

How motivated are trade unions to fight for workplace gender diversity?

Extant studies debate the idea that the lack of necessary conditions for stronger bargaining power lessens the presence of union demands in state decisions (Ertugay, 2013; Sevgi, 2012). After the 2011 elections, the increasing emphasis on family policies rather than women, development of state offices for the support of family, low rates of female trade union participation, exemptions from violent crimes, imprisonment of journalists, media censorship, and intolerance of protests and strikes are reported by various groups including academicians, journalists, and NGOs (Berk & Gumuscu, 2016; Human Rights Watch, 2014; Yılmaz, 2018). In line with these studies and reports, we expect that the influence of patriarchal, conservative notions of gender roles and relations, such as underrepresentation of women in managerial positions, women's reluctance to advance in managerial levels, tendency of assigning domestic responsibilities to women, denial of LGBTQIA+ rights, intolerance towards immigrants and disinterest towards ethnicity, will dominate workplace practices. Indeed, the interview data underscore the conservative character of union managers' manifest patriarchal norms. An argument of an interviewee is as follows:

> There's something in the union management norm that maintains the transfer of roles from father to son. Our previous president was the president for 30 years . . . He was president from there until his death. A male mentality sees himself as the entrepreneur, the manager, the leader and the head. They earn money and distribute it to their male alliances, give individual rewards and share their confessions with each other. They do it at the rakı table. That's why you do not see many women in the union movement.

Interviewees also referred to male dominance in the unions as an important factor in shaping union work and activism, thus making the negligence of diversity management practices in a union context inevitable: "You know the trade unions; everything is based on jobs for men. Some policies are determined only according to the needs of men. In the meantime, whatever the others find for themselves, they get their share".

In terms of exercising gender diversity, interviews in support of the Türer's study (2020) show that women representatives occupying staff positions, on a temporary basis, counsel union executives during collective negotiations and international meetings for gender-specific issues. Furthermore, interviewees claim that Turkish trade unions avoid officially establishing women's commissions, since these councils need to be positioned within the organisational hierarchy and secured with a budget and codes of conduct. Hence, within unions, opportunities are limited to delivering training on gender equality norms and the prevention of harassment issues in the workplace.

> There are no women's commissions in trade unions. . . . A women's commission is defined in the organisational charts as one of the main units of the union. If the women's commissions are not guaranteed by

> the statute of the union, it means that they are not official. . . . What I mean by being guaranteed is; a women's commission must have its own budget. It has to be allocated from the main budget of the union. De facto structures are formed where 3 to 5 women come together. These types of commissions are instrumental for publicity. . . . For example, International Trade Union Confederations are checking for such structures. They show them their organisation charts and say, "Yes, look we also have a women's commission. But this women's commission is not official, does not have a budget or an agenda."

As we discussed in relation to non-governmental organisations, even the ones that are accused of being capital-oriented like TÜSİAD face obstacles in maintaining parity-oriented dialogue with the state and other actors in an authoritarian regime. Thus, the pressures of international organisations are taken as an opportunity to advance steps taken for gender equality in Turkish workplaces (Ergu, 2017). Interviewees support this argument with statements about the ineffectiveness of unions in implementing international standards. It is claimed that, more than unions, pressures of the international organisations and competition compel companies to implement international standards on women's issues. One of the interviewees explained this as such:

> The fight against discrimination, I think it is an important thing to have it written in collective bargaining agreements. Nevertheless, it usually stays on paper. As far as I can see, companies take the international standards and what their rivals do more seriously than their collective bargaining agreements. . . . Therefore, as far as I know, TÜSİAD had something. Like adding something about prevention of child trafficking and gender equality standards to policy statements. It was also due to an international agreement and many TÜSİAD members chose to implement it. It seems to me that the policy statements international organisations make are implemented much more effectively.

Lastly, issues like nursery services, maternity leave and turnover rates, and underrepresented women in management are also shared by unions. However, interview data reveal that most of these concerns have not been internalised, but instead are used to develop a discourse on discrimination and gender equality as a means of influencing union workers and corporate managers to address women's issues. In terms of business relations, practices are limited to collective bargaining negotiations or training programs, at which unions fail to influence companies for gender-sensitive practices.

Intersectional perspectives of trade unions

While discrimination and equal opportunities are the most referenced issues of gender diversity and inclusion in the workplace, women's ethnicity is nonexistent on union agendas. Instead, Kurdish groups and Kurdish political presence are the sole differences that are considered in moderating ethnicity-based management. One interviewee noted:

> What happens is that the issue with the Kurds is more often involved in internal political balances. This does not mean though. That the union tries to prevent discrimination between Kurdish and Turkish workers in a workplace. . . . After the success of Peoples' Democratic Party, Kurdish groups seriously won in local union elections in several regions. In other words, it changed the balances within the union.

In another interview, we observed feminist perspectives, which emphasise concerns about homophobia, violence, and nationalism due to rising authoritarianism and conservatism among male-dominated unions.

> Now we can say that we are even better on women's issues. When it comes to topics such as LGBTQIA+ and Syrians, it is a different story. If you shake these unions, homophobia and nationalism will come out. . . . They do not want to deal with such problems. No union bureaucrat wants to go and deal with harassment in a workplace. He does not want to be confronted, because he is a man too, he is homophobic too. I think it is more difficult to explain the issue to a union bureaucrat than to a workplace CEO.

Research indicates that LGBTQIA+ presence in trade unions is also low. A report of KAOSGL (2021) demonstrates that while membership rates are below 30 percent, members who hide their identity are at 63.6 percent. In addition, this low presence mainly seems to cause contradictory views among union managers, representatives, and counsellors. Unlike the previous quote, these interview data also indicate the presence of a left-wing union environment that acknowledges the discrimination against LGBTQIA+ groups. Interviewees suggested that LGBTQIA+ practices were added to the agenda among unions with the awareness of the growing women's movement. So, members of these unions tend to compare women's issues with that of LGBTQIA+ and minorities. In so doing, interviewees debate the idea that the management of the differences among members in a union is a challenging process since unions are male-dominated. Interestingly, unlike the dialogues about women's presence in the workplace, trade union attention is directed towards transforming the corporate culture and to pressure corporations to add LGBTQIA+-inclusive employment policies. However, discussions and decisions among unions for addressing and exercising LGBTQIA+ practices are limited to collective negotiations with few of the listed corporations. In addition, left-wing unions have internalised these struggles as an accomplishment and as a method for gaining a competitive advantage against other unions.

> We have also made some very advanced adjustments to LGBTQIA+ members both in terms of permission and in terms of money. For example, if it is 5 days marriage leave to people who get married at work and get married normally, we gave the same permission to those who want to live together with their partners. . . . I do not need to mention 8th of March. It is one of the indispensables of us unions. On March 8, sometimes employers want to impose limits. Here, you know, everyone does need to participate. In some instances, we say, let us start from somewhere. Fifteen per cent of the employees must take the day off if they request it. This is even unlimited in some firms. . . . We have also written these items in the negotiations. As part of the 17 May International Day against Homophobia, Transphobia, and Pride Week, there have been regulations regarding the permissions for the friends who want to participate in the activities and events.

Conclusion

Our analysis and the literature about gender practices in Turkish trade unions show that many steps are required to implement gender-sensitive diversity management programs. Furthermore, de-unionisation, financial limitations, and male dominance in the management of the unions as well as the sectors that unions are mostly involved in make the process more challenging. The number of women in Turkish trade unions is at an alarmingly low level, and unions need to provide more motivation for women to join. The lack of data regarding the effect of the pandemic, age, and other surface-level diversity variables is also an important barrier to developing policies and strategies that would enable trade unions to benefit from gender equal environments.

Turkish trade unions also interpret their position in the sectors as too weak to influence corporations in terms of increasing gender presence in managerial roles as well as eliminating the gender gap in income and other vital labour indicators. Thus, similar to the state passing its social responsibilities on to corporations, unions also tend to pass their role of activism and pressure on to international organisations. This is because union members acknowledge that corporations are in a competition towards fulfilling sustainability development goals that involve equal opportunities. Corporations continue to perceive being signatories of international sustainability projects as a competitive advantage. Perhaps, through stronger international agreements, corporations can advance gender diversity. However, more must be done to advance unions for women's presence.

References

Akçay, Ü. (2018). *Neoliberal Populism in Turkey and Its Crisis*. IPE Working Papers 100/2018, Berlin School of Economics and Law, Institute for International Political Economy (IPE). Retrieved from https://ideas.repec.org/p/zbw/ipewps/1002018.html

Aksu, S. (2020). Türk-metal üyesi kadınlar: Eylemler güzel ama konu mankeni değiliz [Turkish Metal member women: Actions are good, but we are not subject models]. *Ekmek ve Gül*. Retrieved from https://ekmekvegul.net/dergi/turk-metal-uyesi-kadinlar-eylemler-guzel-ama-konu-mankeni-degiliz

Akyol, K. (April, 2016). *Gezi'deki polis şiddeti henüz yargılanmadı*. Deutsche Welle Türkçe. Received from www.dw.com/tr/gezideki-polis-per centC5per cent9Fiddeti-henper centC3per centBCz-yargper centC4per centB1lanmadper centC4per centB1/a-19292578

Arıcan, Y. F. (2018). Sınıf, siyaset ve kimlik arasında: Hak-İşçi sendikaları konfederasyonu. In Savaşkan, O., ve Ertan, M. (der.), *Turkey'nin büyük dönüşümü* (pp. 551–577). İletişim.

Baycık, G., Doğan, S., Yangın, D. D., & Yay, O. (2021). COVID 19 pandemisinde uzaktan çalışma: Tespit ve öneriler [Remote work in the COVID-19 pandemic: Detections and recommendations]. *Çalışma ve Toplum*, 3(70), 1683–1728. Retrieved from https://calismatoplum.org/makale/covid-19-pandemisinde-uzaktan-calisma-tespit-ve-oneriler-1

Berk, E., & Gumuscu, S. (2016). Rising competitive authoritarianism in Turkey. *Third World Quarterly*, 37(9), 1581–1606. https://doi.org/10.1080/01436597.2015.1135732

Birelma, A. (2021). Turkey'de sendikal hareketin ve hakların yukarıdan görünümü: Niteliksel bir araştırma [A view of the trade union movement and rights from above in Turkey: A qualitative research]. *Çalışma ve Toplum*, 69(3), 1839–1870. Retrieved from https://calismatoplum.org/makale/turkiyede-sendikal-hareketin-ve-haklarin-yukaridan-gorunumu-niteliksel-bir-arastirma

Bonacini, L., Gallo, G., & Scicchitano, S. (2021). Working from home and income inequality: Risks of a "new normal" with COVID-19. *Journal of Population Economics*, 34(1), 303–360. https://doi.org/10.1007/s00148-020-00800-7

Cam, E. (2019). *Social Dialogue and Democracy in the Workplace: Trade Union and Employer Perspectives from Turkey*. Springer.

Çelik, A. (2015). Turkey's new labour regime under the Justice and Development Party in the first decade of the twenty-first century: Authoritarian flexibilization. *Middle Eastern Studies*, 51(4), 618–635. https://doi.org/10.1080/00263206.2014.987665

Çoban, B. (2013). Sendikal örgütlenmede yeni deneyimler ve değişen stratejiler [New experiences and changing strategies in union organizing]. *Çalışma ve Toplum*, 38, 375–412. Retrieved from www.calismatoplum.org/makale/sendikal-orgutlenmede-yeni-deneyimler-ve-degisen-stratejiler

DİSK. (2022a). *DİSK tarihi cilt 1: Kuruluş direniş varoluş* [DISK History Volume 1: Establishment Resistance Existence]. Retrieved from http:/arastirma.disk.org.tr/wp-content/uploads/2022/02/disk-tarihi-1-cilt-2-baski-2022.pdf

DİSK. (2022b). *DİSK tarihi cilt 2: Kuruluş direniş varoluş* [DISK History Volume 2: Solidarity Resistance Hope]. Retrieved from http:/arastirma.disk.org.tr/wp-content/uploads/2022/02/DISK-Tarihi-1-Cilt-2-Baski-2022.pdf

Ercan, F., & Oğuz, Ş. (2015). From Gezi resistance to Soma massacre: Capital accumulation and class struggle in Turkey. *Socialist Register*, 51(1), 114–135.

Ekmek ve Gül. (2022). Türk metal üyesi binlerce işçi MESS'in sefalet zammı dayatmasına karşı mitingde [Thousands of Turkish metal member workers rally against MESS's imposition of misery hikes]. *Ekmek ve Gül*. Retrieved from https://ekmekvegul.net/gundem/turk-metal-uyesi-binlerce-isci-messin-sefalet-zammi-dayatmasina-karsi-mitingde

Ergu, E. (2017, March). Olağan ve yapıcı gündemi özlüyoruz [We miss the ordinary and constructive agenda]. *Hürriyet*. Retrieved from www.hurriyet.com.tr/ekonomi/olagan-ve-yapici-gundemi-ozluyoruz-40406265

Ertugay, F. (2013). Bir çelişki ve gerilim alanı olarak işçi örgütleri-devlet ilişkisi ve sivil toplum retoriği [Workers' organizations-state relationship and civil society rhetoric as an area of contradiction and tension]. *Hak İş Uluslararası Emek ve Toplum Dergisi*, 2(3), 44–65.

ETUC. (2021). *Recommendations on Engaging Young People in Trade Unions*. Retrieved from www.etuc.org/en/publication/engaging-young-people-trade-unions

Evrensel. (2021). *MESS sözleşmesinde sefalete imza attılar* [Signing Misery in the MESS Contract]. Retrieved from www.evrensel.net/haber/452477/mess-sozlesmesinde-sefalete-imza-attilar-isciler-yuzde-50-istedi-sendikalar-yuzde-27-44e-evet-dedi?a=v4ZP

Gök, M. (2021). HAK-İŞ ve siyaset [HAK-İŞ and politics]. *Hak İş Uluslararası Emek ve Toplum Dergisi*, 10(27), 214–235. https://doi.org/10.31199/hakisderg.939204

Gökçe, A. (2021). Endüstri ilişkileri iklimi ve COVID-19 pandemi sürecinin yansımaları [Industrial relations climate and reflections of the COVID-19 pandemic process]. *Gümüşhane Üniversitesi Sosyal Bilimler Dergisi*, 12(2), 665–678. Retrieved from https://dergipark.org.tr/en/pub/gumus/issue/62554/901438

Human Rights Watch. (2014). *Turkey's Human Rights Rollback*. HRW.

ILO. (2022a). Statistics on collective barganing. *International Labour Organisation*. Retrieved from https://ilostat.ilo.org/topics/collective-bargaining/.

ILO. (2022b). Statistics on union membership. *International Labour Organisation*. Retrieved from https://ilostat.ilo.org/topics/union-membership/

KAOSGL. (2021). *Turkey'de kamu çalışanı lezbiyen, gey, biseksüel, trans, interseks ve artılarındurumu: 2021 yılı araştırması* [Status of Public Employees Lesbian, Gay, Bisexual,

Trans, Intersex and Pros in Turkey: The Year 2021 Survey]. Received from https://dspace.ceid.org.tr/xmlui/bitstream/handle/1/2004/kamu21-1.pdf?sequence=1&isAllowed=y

Keleş, D. (2018). Türkiye'de sendika kadın ilişkisi: Sendikacı kadınların bakış açılarına ilişkin bir değerlendirme [Union-women relationship in Turkey: An evaluation of the perspectives of unionist women]. *Çalışma ve Toplum*, 59(4). Retrieved from www.calismatoplum.org/makale/turkiyede-sendika-kadiniliskisi-sendikacikadinlarin-bakisacilarinailiskin-bir-degerlendirme

Keleş, D. (2020). *Sendikalarda toplumsal cinsiyet eşitliğini sağlamanın bir aracı olarak kadın komiteleri: Hak-İş kadın komitesine içerden bakış* [Women's Committees as a Tool to Ensure Gender Equality in Unions: Insider View of Hak-İş Women's Committee]. *Genel-İş Emek Araştırma Dergisi* (GEAD), 191. https://search.trdizin.gov.tr/yayin/detay/413744/sendikalarda-toplumsal-cinsiyet-esitligini-saglamanin-bir-araci-olarak-kadin-komiteleri-hak-is-kadin-komitesine-icerden-bakis

Kopuk, B. M., & Taşoğulları, G. (2019). Çalışma yaşamında kadın ve sendika ilişkisi [Relationship between women and unions in working life]. *Fırat Üniversitesi Uluslararası İktisadi ve İdari Bilimler Dergisi*, 3(1), 75–90. Retrieved from https://dergipark.org.tr/en/pub/fuuiibfdergi/issue/46079/579631

Meçik, O., & Aytun, U. (2020). COVID-19 döneminde eşitsizlikler: Çalışma içerikleri ve ücretler [Inequalities in the COVID-19 era: Work content and wages]. *Emek Araştırma Dergisi*, 11, 1–26. Retrieved from http://www.emekarastirma.org/uploads/dergi/2993.pdf

OECD. (2022). *Trade Union Dataset*. Retrieved from https://stats.oecd.org/Index.aspx?DataSetCode=TUD

Önder, N. (2016). *The Economic Transformation of Turkey: Neoliberalism and State Intervention*. London: I.B. Tauris.

Özbilgin, M. F. (2015). Farklılık yönetimi: Özel sayıya giriş [Diversity management: Introduction to special issue]. *Yönetim Araştırmaları Dergisi*, 12(1–2), 7–8. Retrieved from http://yad.baskent.edu.tr/files/2015_cilt_12_1.pdf

Özbilgin, M. F., & Slutskaya, N. (2017). Consequences of neo-liberal politics on equality and diversity at work in Britain: Is resistance futile? In Chanlat, J.-F., & Özbligin, M. F. (Eds.), *Management and Diversity* (*International Perspectives on Equality, Diversity and Inclusion*) (Vol. 4, pp. 319–334). Emerald Publishing Limited. https://doi.org/10.1108/S2051-233320160000004015

Özbilgin, M. F., & Yalkın, C. (2019). Hegemonic dividend and workforce diversity: The case of "biat" and meritocracy in nation branding in Turkey. *Journal of Management & Organization*, 25(4), 543–553. https://doi.org/10.1017/jmo.2019.39

Özdemir, A. M., & Yücesan-Özdemir, G. (2006). Labour law reform in Turkey in the 2000s: The devil is not in detail but in the legal texts too. *Economic and Industrial Democracy*, 27(2), 311–331 https://doi.org/10.1177/0143831X06060592

Sevgi, H. (2012). Neo-liberalizme karşı sendikal mücadele: Toplumsal hareket sendikacılığı [Trade union struggle against neo-liberalism: Social movement unionism]. *Ekonomi Bilimleri Dergisi*, 4(2). Retrieved from https://dergipark.org.tr/en/pub/ebd/issue/4860/66856

Tabak, H., & Doğan, M. (2022). Global gender equality norm and trade unions in Turkey: Local contestations, rival validations, and discrepant receptions. *Journal of Political Sciences*, 31(1), 53–72. https://doi.org/10.26650/siyasal.2022.31.947376

TOKAD. (2011). *Neoliberal dönemde sendikacılık ve sendikalar* [Unionism and Trade Unions in the Neoliberal Era]. Retrieved from www.tokad.org/2011/08/04/neoliberal-donemde-sendikacilik-ve-sendikalar/

Tokat, B., & Aslan, Ö. (2009). *Neoliberal politika karşısında geleneksel sendika modelinin çıkmazları üzerine Betül Urhan ile söyleşi* [Interview with Betül Urhan on the Dilemmas of the Traditional Union Model in the Face of Neoliberal Politics]. *Feminist Yaklaşımlar*. Received from www.feministyaklasimlar.org/sayi-08-haziran-2009/neoliberal-sistem-karsisinda/

Türer, A. (2020). *Türkiye'deki üye sendikalarda kadın temsili ve kadına yönelik faaliyetler haritalama çalışması* [Representation of Women in Member Unions in Turkey and Activities for Mapping]. Retrieved July 10, 2022, from https://dspace.ceid.org.tr/xmlui/handle/1/903

Urhan, B. (2017). Sendika içi demokrasi ve sendika içi kadın örgütlenmesi. *Journal of Social Policy Conferences*, 29–58. Retrieved from https://dergipark.org.tr/en/pub/iusskd/issue/33251/370114

Yildirim, T. M., & Eslen-Ziya, H. (2021). The differential impact of COVID-19 on the work conditions of women and men academics during the lockdown. *Gender, Work & Organisation*, 28, 243–249.

Yılmaz, Z. (2018). The AKP and the new politics of the social: Fragile citizenship, authoritarian populism and paternalist family policies. In *Populism and the Crisis of Democracy* (pp. 150–167). Routledge.

Yılmaz, Z., & Turner, B. S. (2019). Turkey's deepening authoritarianism and the fall of electoral democracy. *British Journal of Middle Eastern Studies*, 46(5), 691–698. https://doi.org/10.1080/13530194.2019.1642662

7 Listed companies

Never-ending training and an awareness-raising fetish

Introduction

Today, gender diversity programs are very popular among listed Turkish companies. Listed companies compete to show how gender-friendly they are through their websites, media outlets, and various platforms supported within business circles.

The introduction of gender diversity practices by listed companies in Turkey is triggered mainly by external stakeholders. Though some of the managers we interviewed stated that they were willing to initiate diversity and inclusion programs in companies on their own as an individual practice long before the "gender diversity wave", they stated that it is not fair to expect them to do so. Internal dynamics, social facts, realities like economic crises, and the pandemic that the business sectors face and legal obligations all limit the advancement of these programs. Thus, to comprehend Turkish diversity management, it is vital to examine the responses from the managers and understand the pressures they face in the institutional environment (Ali, 2016; Yang & Konrad, 2011; Pitts et al., 2010).

When we investigated Turkish listed companies to find out how gender-inclusive programs spread in the Turkish business environment, we found that interviewees mainly attributed the initiation of the programs to the Equality in the Workplace Platform. One of the human resources directors described this as follows:

> We made some preparations within the scope of that platform. We actually focused a bit around our commitments. . . . Then, an informative presentation was made to the board of directors about the platform; the purpose of the platform, its establishment stage, our commitments, and the results of the survey conducted by the ministry. Our action plan was accepted on the basis of it. Afterwards, we became a member of the platform.

DOI: 10.4324/9781003244868-8

Most of the company managers mentioned more or less the same methods, their commitments, action plans, etc. However, these commitments are not legally binding. Accordingly, UN WEP also triggered social demand and awareness with its Declaration of Equality, which states 11 principles[1] to support women's workforce participation and to determine the basic standards of equality in the workplace. Even though the Platform is inactive at the moment, signatory companies still address these principles on their websites. An interviewee talked about equality in the workplace and WEPs principles as follows:

> The private sector is especially focused on diversity in Turkey and inclusion programs have actually entered the agenda of companies of small to large scale . . . the United Nations Global Compact, UN Woman's Women Empowerment Principles, for example, was signed in many companies. . . . The company does not enter into any obligation signing it. However, first, it offers you a good framework if you are concerned about where to start or what to do with gender equality. It has its own guide . . . if you truly want to implement gender equality in a company."

Over time, diversity management evolved into a field where companies competed for reputation; they were motivated to win the championship at gender equality and continued inclusion projects.

Diversity beyond gender

When we studied the literature and examined the countries where the diversity approach originated, we could see that the right representation of diversity was based not only on gender but also on ethnicities (Syed & Özbilgin, 2019; Colgan, 2011). In essence, such an approach reflects a human rights perspective. In other words, if a group is represented systematically at a much lower rate as compared to others and has been left in a disadvantageous position, business activities have to be monitored by specific mechanisms like quota systems or legal requirements (Hills, 2015). In many countries, diversity quotas are used to combat discrimination for groups that are disadvantaged because of their surface-level differences. For instance, in North American countries, quotas for ethnic minorities in higher education are very common. Various diversity quotas have also been introduced in European countries to combat the underrepresentation of minority groups in the workplace (Takagi & Gröschl 2012).

In Turkey, although there are diverse groups in terms of ethnicity, religious sects, and sexual orientation, companies do not recognise these surface-level differences. Instead, they tend to focus only on gender equality issues and women's rights. One of the interviewees stated that:

> When we say diversity, we ignore ethnicity. We already have one of the biggest ethnic groups, Kurds, and we also have Laz and Cerkez people. There's no pressure we feel to identify them. So, we find it more sincere to think of it as not diversity, but rather as a matter of male and female.

The quota application for hiring the disabled is widely applied in European countries by means of law for people with disabilities (PwD). For example, since 1987, France has imposed a 6 percent disability quota for firms with 20 or more employees. Similarly, the PwD quota for companies with more than 20 employees in Germany is 5 percent (Gröschl & Takagi, 2016). The quota application for the disabled in Turkey is regulated in Article 30 of Labour Law No. 4857. Accordingly, it is obligatory to employ 3 percent PwD in private sector workplaces employing 50 or more workers, 4 percent in public workplaces, and 2 percent for ex-convicts or those injured in the fight against terrorism. Another interviewee confirmed the absence of different segments in diversity and inclusion programs: "Companies in Turkey are only interested in gender diversity. The situation in legal regulations is not very bright either. . . . Some companies do not want to employ people with disabilities."

There are gender diversity quota applications developed for different institutions. The most common examples of this today are the regulatory quotas for female candidates in political positions (Gröschl & Takagi, 2016). The United States also has very effective diversity tools especially for ethnic and racial groups and gender division (Farndale et al., 2015). Although all these tools are based on legal requirements, companies publicise their implementations voluntarily (Plitmann, 2022). One of our interviewees, who has attended several UN meetings, stated that quota and other legal adjustments are a necessity for equality in the workplace.

> Change is not possible without quotas and laws. This is a topic discussed at UN panels every year. Last year, for example, there was the German Minister of Labour, a person from the right-wing party who had heavily argued against the quota for years until he got involved and realised the necessity of quotas. In other words, even in countries with advanced equality labour laws compared to other countries, such as Germany, you cannot have gender quotas; you cannot go one-step further. The Australian prime minister said the same thing. In other words, they are the most developed countries in the world in terms of many human rights. Because there is a quota system in Scandinavian countries.

Compliance with law

As a result of neoliberal policies in Western democracies, the state passed its regulatory responsibility for ensuring equality and diversity at work to big companies. (Tatli, 2011; Özbilgin & Slutskaya, 2017; Özbilgin & Tatli, 2011). Most theoretical frames of diversity management are developed in countries where there are strong legal regulations as well as normative rules and a supportive diversity discourse (Özbilgin, et al., 2016). On the other hand, there are increasing cases of deregulation and volunteerism and resistance to protective legislations internationally. Küskü et al. (2021) identifies Turkey as a country that suffers a toxic triangle: deregulated labour markets where equality laws are almost absent, where voluntarism is encouraged without responsibility, and where there are thriving impediments against diversity discourse. Thus, we can say that in Turkey, legislation that endorses equality is very lenient. Although most of the listed companies limit their gender diversity practices to legal obligations, the Turkish legal system is far from being equipped to support diversity and equality at the workplace. One of the HR managers stated that:

> Every country needs to make legal arrangements on the subject. In other words, some laws and regulations have to be established. . . . Just as companies have to employ a certain percentage of people with disabilities. There should be legally binding rules for increasing the number of women employees at every level.

The legal side of gender diversity practices is crucial for framing inclusive practices. However, there are some other barriers for women's labour force participation in Turkey. Lack of affordable childcare services is one of the major problems that women face in the workplace. The literature highlights the inadequate supply of public childcare services and the high price of private childcare services as being among the most important reasons for women with children to withdraw from employment (Akkan & Serim, 2018, Kazanoğlu, 2019, Ulutaş, 2015). It is a great challenge, especially for women who work in low-wage jobs or who work informally for wages under minimum wage levels. While the labour force participation rate of women with small children in Turkey is 24 percent, this rate is 34 percent for women who do not have children. Moreover, in Turkey, the rate of women with care responsibilities in informal employment is 42 percent, while this rate is 62 percent for those who do not have care responsibilities (ILO, 2018). Studies have demonstrated that women's care responsibilities cause women to leave the labour market or to choose informal work. With the institutionalisation of these services, more women might be able to be employed, and it might be possible for women in the paid care sector to work in safe and secure ways. Furthermore, Turkish society still values patriarchal norms that define the woman's role as caregiver, justify strong family control over women (Gündüz-Hoşgör & Smits, 2008), and influence women's participation in the labour force. It is also still common among working women to leave their children with family elders for care (TÜİK, 2017). Thus, existing childcare norms (relying on family members as caregivers), patriarchal culture, and poor working conditions strengthen gendered role prescriptions (Kolaşın et al., 2015).

According to Turkish regulations on Working Conditions of Pregnant or Nursing Women, Nursing Rooms and Child Care Dormitories, businesses that employ more than 150 female workers are obliged to open a nursery. However, in Turkey, there are only a few employers who provide such services for their employees. Employees are well aware of this situation, but they still do not consider the provision of childcare services as the employer's responsibility. Instead, they assume this to be a state responsibility or sometimes approach municipalities for solutions. Listed companies are easily avoiding this legislation since sanctions, control mechanisms, and enforcement laws are weak. Thus, listed companies in most of the cases do not provide childcare services for their employees because they can easily avoid their responsibilities. The HR director of one of the biggest firms in Turkey stated that they provide childcare services only at one plant where it is necessary to employ a special group of women to assemble a special type of sensitive electric circuit. For the rest of their plants, they do not provide childcare services. She stated, "I have never seen state agencies monitoring childcare services. Even if it is inspected, there is no point in providing childcare services for firms because fines are very low when they do not comply with the regulations".

Other frequently mentioned barriers for women's participation in the labour force are mobbing and sexual harassment. The main issue is that women are often left by employers to deal with the legal procedures on their own. Only a few of the interviewees mentioned this issue and provided some evidence about their preventive practices. The reason for this neglect is explained as such:

> When the person who has been mobbed or harassed makes a complaint to the prosecutor's office a very frustrating process begins. She needs to go to court, she will get some reports and, if the company does not support her, it is very difficult for that woman to win the case. She will only be successful if the company stands by her. So, mobbing and harassment

should be addressed in the company's ethical code. . . . Companies have to bear the costs and time losses of these people.

"Too soft" human resources practices

When we asked HR directors of the leading corporations about their policies and practices on diversity, they mainly spoke about their ongoing training activities. It is almost an automatic response when companies are asked what they are doing. Why? Because training sessions are excellent window dressing, one of the less-costly solutions for companies to use to promote their gender-friendly environments to stakeholders. Training is framed as the viable solution to raise awareness among their employees, as if in year 2022 employees are still not aware of women's issues in the workplace. Furthermore, it is a safe practice for HR personnel to show their managers that they actually perform work and fulfil their responsibilities. These managers still argue that they have the role to transform their value system and company culture for a more egalitarian gender relation. However, it seems to be just the talk of the practice. There is no effective action. None of the companies we interviewed attempted to move beyond the legal requirements. An HR director explained training activities in a detailed way:

> In the first place, a corporate culture and perception survey regarding the place of women in the company was conducted. By means of this study, a perception analysis was complemented within the company. . . . First of all, together with our consulting firm, the training program entitled "I am at work, and I can balance" was designed and delivered. All employees attended these training sessions. The purpose of the training was to describe living as a whole that would enable all individuals to find a balance between their work, family, and themselves. After that, we started awareness and self-confidence trainings, "high heel sounds on the way to success". . . . A role-play was made for all employees to develop empathy skills. It was an awareness program, and then we started a more specific, private coaching program for our women managers.

Most of the managers assumed that it was a woman's individual responsibility to become successful at work. So, instead of changing the conditions, they tried to change women's attitudes towards their careers. If she failed, the woman was expected to admit that her failure was related to either a lack of motivation or a lack of self-confidence. Managers also talk about training programs that aim to change the perceptions of male employees towards women or to increase the motivation and confidence of the women, as if women have never been confident enough to be managers. Moreover, companies are also eager to extend training activities outside their companies and conduct training activities for their constituencies as well.

Other than these "too soft" practices, there are some other implementations that could help increase the number of women in companies and the number of women managers and directors. In fact, leading companies try to integrate practices in line with their commitments. They define equal opportunity criteria for men and women in human resources policies. These criteria differ from one company to another. An HR manager of a big holding company that operates mainly in the service sector explained his actions on this issue as follows:

> Increasing the rate of female employees was among our commitments but I have to say that there was no targeted rate or quota. When we started in 2012, our rate of women employees was 24–25 percent, after 6 years this ratio rose to 35 percent. 50 percent of newly recruited employees are now women. What are we doing specifically? For example, for all promotions, we recruit a women candidate. We try to choose a woman candidate if there are co-candidates. In this way we were able to achieve equality in recruitment. In appointments to managerial positions, we propose three candidates, one of them must be a woman. This is our company rule.

Although many HR managers that we interviewed talked about similar practices, progress was very limited in terms of both the number of female employees and the number of women in managerial positions for the last decade since diversity practices entered Turkey's agenda. While a certain improvement was observed in companies that invested in sectors where women work more in terms of their field of activity, there was a negligible improvement, especially in large companies that invested mainly in industry. The manager of a company which is among the largest holdings in Turkey and defines itself as a diversity champion explained the point they have reached in terms of gender equality in their companies.

> There is no possibility of a solution without a quota, but unfortunately, I do not see the possibility of a quota in Turkey anytime soon. That's why all of our efforts are at least helpful so that it doesn't get worse. Plus, the creation of at least an awareness on this issue, that is, thinking twice, ensures that a manager is careful when making an appointment and hiring staff. I hope we are paving the way for future generations

> and girls. But that's how we started this project, we came from here to there, so we don't see much of its reflection in the results. If it wasn't, it might have been worse.

Although HR managers claimed that they were implementing an equal wage policy for women and men, studies on Turkey report that women earn less than men for the same job (for example, Akhmedjonov, 2012; ILO, 2021).

Diversity or corporate social responsibility?

In Turkey, gender diversity became a social responsibility activity, and listed companies declared women-related projects in their social responsibility and sustainability reports. "Gender diversity and inclusion are taken as core values" said the communication director of one of the biggest Turkish conglomerates.

Sustainability, as a trend that started about 15 years ago, influenced Turkish business circles. Since then, listed companies have started to publish sustainability reports. These companies integrated sustainability as a performance criterion, measured it, and prepared sustainability reports (Özçelik et al., 2015; Kocamiş & Yildirim, 2016; Caymaz et al., 2014). The communications director of a listed company claimed that "gender issues are related to sustainability and comes after ecology". Currently, the Turkish business world considers the issue of sustainability and thus gender diversity as "a hot and cool field", and listed companies try to integrate these issues into their processes of recruitment and promotion (Ozdora-Aksak & Atakan-Duman, 2016). In so doing, they create a corporate image and reputation. In other words, the image created becomes more important than the actual practice.

Constituencies other than the listed companies contribute to this image- and reputation-building process. For example, some business magazines, such as Capital, organise contests to identify "women-friendly companies" (for details, see Capital, 2022). Similarly, PERYÖN awards a company every year for its performance on diversity and inclusion management (HR Dergi, 2022; PERYÖN, n.d). One of the HR managers that we interviewed stated that gender diversity is very important for the company's visibility.

> In Turkey, the public relations side of gender diversity is more important. When public relations come to the fore, the race begins. I did it, I did the best. . . . But the aim here should be to spread diversity practices throughout the whole country, but it is more important for companies to have news on a television program, a magazine or in printed media.

From all these arguments, we can conclude that listed companies tend to develop projects as a public relations activity, instead of developing practices to promote diversity generally and gender diversity specifically within their companies to support women or young women students. In other words, rather than improving working conditions and providing opportunities for their employees, the HR departments of these companies focus on corporate social responsibility activities to support women outside their own companies. It is common belief among Turkish business circles that "gender equality" advances creativity and innovation by attracting a talented workforce and improving quality. Thus, companies mainly base their principles on the perspective of the utilisation of human capital rather than human rights. An interviewee from a listed company stated that, "their main concern is to help women to participate fully in economic life both vertically and horizontally throughout all levels of economic activity for a stronger and sustainable economy".

Considering women's role in buying decisions, companies also started to attract women consumers by means of gender diversity projects (Lu et al., 2020). Thus, gender diversity projects are considered a tool to reach women consumers. We have observed a similar attitude among the managers of Turkish listed companies. "If this is a woman-friendly company, so if I integrate the woman more and reflect it into my brand, it will also contribute more to our reputation and brand."

Women in the upper echelons

Women are absent from the upper echelons of public firms in Turkey. According to the results of the household labour force survey; the rate of women in senior and middle management positions in companies was 14.4 percent in 2012 and rose to 19.3 percent in 2020 (TUIK, 2022). Our earlier study, that was based on the 2015 BİST data, indicated that women directors held only 3 percent of CEO positions, 11 percent of board seats, and 10.8 percent of board positions (Özsoy et al., 2021).

Attaining gender diversity on boards of directors is one of the most important aspects of gender diversity projects for the listed firms in many western countries. After the global economic crisis of 2008, the issue of increasing the number of women on corporate boards gained immense international attention (Sun et al., 2015). Accordingly, there has been pressure from a diverse set of constituencies, such as the European Commission, regulators, political parties, NGOs, and investors to increase the number of women on corporate boards. Although in 2012 regulations concerning board structure and function were disseminated by the Turkish government, unlike many EU countries (Syzdlo, 2015), the new Turkish law did not introduce gender quotas for women members. The Capital Markets Board of Turkey (CMBT) also updated corporate governance principles in 2011, and the new principles suggested that listed companies should include at least "one women director" in their boardroom. However, this principle does not have any mandatory power.

Considering nomination of female candidates, the Turkish business community is not very responsive. As one of the male interviewees, stated, "On the business side there is 'a lack of demand' for women directors. Most of the time they are not able to understand why there is a need for such an issue". Thus, it seems that the Turkish business community is reluctant to respond positively unless mandatory measures are taken by the CMBT. As stated by a male interviewee:

> The Turkish business community's board gender diversity perspective is very shallow. . . . They are opposed to a quota system. They believe it would bring inequality for the potential candidates. . . . Turkey's primary instrument in improving gender diversity in corporate boards is the CMBT's Corporate Governance Guidelines and without a mandatory quota system it is impossible to increase the number of women on Turkish Corporate Boards.

However, board gender diversity has not been an institutionalised practice on the Turkish corporate governance landscape. The human resources director of a holding company stated this issue in this way:

> When we initiated our diversity program, board gender diversity advocates tried to force us to increase the number of women board members, however we have a long way to go to reach that stage. In our company we started a long-term project. We are planting the seeds today; only in the long run can we increase the number of directors and executives.

These initiatives suggest that equality ought to be promoted through community initiatives by means of various stakeholders. Although many companies have extensive programs for gender equality, they claim that "they are not ready to increase the number of women directors on company boards for the near future because there are not enough candidates for such positions". It seems that business as well as government and civil society organisations prefer voluntary initiatives and self-regulatory company codes that reflect the dominant market-friendly neoliberal normative framework over legal or regulatory action.

Conclusion

The aim of this chapter was to provide a detailed analysis of the diversity management practices of listed companies. We tried to identify themes that were expressed by interviewees, such as equal opportunities, work-life balance, training programs, legal compliance mechanisms, board and managerial diversity, and gender roles and nursery services, as well as concerns about obstacles deriving from societal assumptions and board and state disinterest in advancing women's managerial positions. In addition to analysing the discourse adopted by these firms, the chapter also explored the actions taken, such as establishing departments for gender issues, public relations activities, and recruiting and promoting women for managerial positions.

As can be seen in the following example, a holding that pioneered gender diversity in Turkey, after almost ten years of efforts, has still not been able to create a radical change within the company:

> X Holding is one of the leading gender equality "advocates" in the Turkish business world. Aiming for equal representation at every level and in every business category for gender equality, X Holding focuses on eliminating the perceptions of traditional role distribution and creating gender-sensitive workplaces. Within the scope of gender equality activities, the company organises awareness programs for 95,000 employees, 10 thousand dealers and suppliers, and supports the emergence and dissemination of successful examples. The markedly low rate of women's participation in employment in Turkey is also reflected in X Group companies. It has reached a significant part of Turkey in terms of the sectors in which it operates and the number of employees and can set an example for the country's progress in this field.
>
> X Holding, started its work on gender equality with the signing of the Equality at Work Declaration in 2013. In 2015 the Women's Empowerment Principles, the joint text of UN Women's Unit and the UN Global Compact were signed. X Holding was selected as among the top 10 Impact Champions on a global level as part of the HeForShe Project carried out by the UN Women. The percentages of women as a total number of employees, new hires, senior management and on the Board of Directors are regularly monitored and shared in the global HeforShe reports. During the studies, it has been determined that the distinction between women's work and men's work is a problem area that needs to be solved in some sectors where the Group operates. There is a need for action in these sectors to transform perceptions of gender stereotypes and initiate exemplary practices.
>
> In 2015, "I Support Gender Equality for My Country Project" was launched with the support of senior management. The project aims to be a role model in adopting an egalitarian approach in business culture and social life, as well as raising awareness of the causes and consequences of gender inequality in X Group and the entire society. Within the scope of the project, which was carried out with the active participation of

> 350 employees and 118 dealer volunteers in X Group, action was taken to create a perception change by organising gender equality seminars. It was also aimed at reaching local stakeholders (youth, public employees, employers) through dealers and to provide information on gender equality.
>
> Seminars for senior management, employees and dealers were organised in cooperation with universities and NGOs. In the first period of the project, 80 percent of the employees were reached. It was planned that the dealership work would continue until the end of 2017 and that all employees would attend the seminars. Participants in seminars and workshops were expected to develop projects to transform their workplaces on the axis of gender equality, in line with the needs of their companies. It was intended to disseminate successful projects within the Community.
>
> Another important part of the X Group's sphere of influence is the communication efforts of X brands. Communication activities are carried out every day, addressing women, men and families through many different channels, through brands with powerful communication platforms and tools in different sectors. In this context, marketing and communication teams and the agencies that X Group companies work with play an important role in changing gender stereotypes. With this foresight, a guide entitled "Gender Equality in Communication" is being prepared to create a change in communication studies that bring traditional role distribution to large masses. In the light of this guide, workshops are organised for corporate communication, brand and marketing teams in X Group companies and nearly 40 agencies with which companies collaborate in the fields of advertising, social media communication, public relations and event management.

It is evident that many public companies, which are known as the pioneers in the field, also avoid explaining what they are doing in their own companies in terms of diversity management. For example, few of these companies mention the change in the number of female employees or the change in the number of women in management positions. As we mentioned in previous chapters, the initiation of the gender diversity programs in big Turkish companies mainly started after the "equality in the workplace" project. Though the project ended, many companies that started programs are still active in the field. However, their approach is very pragmatic most of the time. Many HR managers and communication directors who are responsible for diversity projects stated that it is a tool to communicate with wider audiences in society. They are aware of the importance of appearing to be a "women friendly company" for both marketing purposes and the reputation of their company. Moreover, when we examined gender diversity discourse in Turkish business circles, they are advocating a diversity approach that aims to increase efficiency and performance in business. So, such an approach is also rather pragmatic.

The availability of accessible and quality care services is crucial for decent work for women. On the basis of social justice, availability of these services decreases the burden of care on women. Thus, women would be able to participate in the workforce at a higher rate. With the institutionalisation of these services, women would be able to be employed in different sectors and male-dominated occupations, even in lower-paid jobs. However, Turkish companies are able to easily avoid their responsibilities as a result of the underregulated labour market that is characterised by a lack of legislation and legal enforcement. Other important barriers to women's labour force participation are sexual harassment and mobbing. Again, women are underprotected by regulations, and most of the time, companies avoid their ethical responsibilities and do not stand by women who are the victims of such immoral conduct.

It seems that, although Turkish companies have taken some important steps towards gender diversity, they have not gotten to the root of the problem of women's employment. Companies aim to improve their reputation and increase their social prestige through diversity programs. Although there are many steps to be taken within the company, they often try to make themselves visible through activities such as mentoring and training programs for women through social projects. Thus, the results show that neither the discourse nor the actions taken have sufficient impact to redress the gender gap in these workplaces.

Notes

1. The Articles of the Declaration of Equality
    1. We respect human rights. We treat all our employees with the basic principle of equality.
    2. We ensure the health, safety and welfare of our female and male employees, regardless of gender.
    3. We specifically support women's participation in the workforce.
    4. We define equal opportunity criteria for men and women in all our human resources policies.
    5. We act and follow the equal pay policy for equal work.
    6. We establish the necessary mechanisms for equal use of career opportunities.
    7. We create and monitor education policies and pay special attention to the participation of women.
    8. We create a working environment and practices that protect the work-family life balance.
    9. We announce developments regarding our equal opportunity plans and achievements through internal and external communication.
    10. We ensure that the statement is disseminated throughout our sphere of influence (our partners, suppliers).
    11. We form a leadership team in our institution to follow up on the issues included in the declaration.

References

Akhmedjonov, A. (2012). New evidence on pay gap between men and women in Turkey. *Economics Letters*, 117(1), 32–34. https://doi.org/10.1016/j.econlet.2012.04.070

Akkan, B., & Serim, S. (2018). Work and family reconciliation in Turkey: Young women as a vulnerable group in the labour market. *Research and Policy on Turkey*, 3(2), 173–186. https://doi.org/10.1080/23760818.2018.1517450

Ali, M. (2016). Impact of gender-focused human resource management on performance: The mediating effects of gender diversity. *Australian Journal of Management*, 41(2), 376–397. https://doi.org/10.1177/0312896214565119

Capital. (2022). *"Kadın dostu şirketler" ödüllerini aldı* ["Women Friendly Companies" Received Awards]. Retrieved from www.capital.com.tr/capital-tv/tum-videolar/kadin-dostu-sirketler-odullerini-aldi

Caymaz, E., Saran, S., & Erenel, F. (2014). The relationship in between corporate sustainability and corporate social responsibility in business: Global compact Turkey. *Journal of Management Marketing and Logistics*, 1(3), 208–217.

Colgan, F. (2011), Equality, diversity and corporate responsibility: Sexual orientation and diversity management in the UK private sector. *Equality, Diversity and Inclusion*, 30(8), 719–734. https://doi.org/10.1108/02610151111183225

Farndale, E., Biron, M., Briscoe, D. R., & Raghuram, S. (2015). A global perspective on diversity and inclusion in work organizations. *The International Journal of Human Resource Management*, 26(6), 677–687. https://doi.org/10.1080/09585192.2014.991511

Gröschl, S., & Takagi, J. (2016). *Diversity quotas, diverse perspectives: The case of gender.* Routledge. https://doi.org/10.4324/9781315577739

Gündüz-Hoşgör, A., & Smits, J. (2008). Variation in labor market participation of married women in Turkey. *Women's Studies International Forum*, 31(2), 104–117. https://doi.org/10.1016/j.wsif.2008.03.003

Hills, J. (2015). Addressing gender quotas in South Africa: Women empowerment and gender equality legislation. *Deakin Law Review*, 20, 153.

HR Dergi. (2022). *PERYÖN: Atılan her adım insana değer!* [PERYÖN: Every Step Taken is Worth Human!]. Retrieved from https://hrdergi.com/peryon-atilan-her-adim-insana-deger

ILO. (2018). *Care Work and Care Jobs for the Future of Decent Work.* Retrieved from www.ilo.org/global/publications/books/WCMS_633135/lang-en/index.htm

ILO. (2021). *Kurumlar arası iş birlikleri ile kadın istihdamını desteklemek: Erken çocukluk bakımı ve eğitimi uygulamaları* [Supporting Women's Employment Through Inter-Institutional Collaborations: Early Childhood Care and Education Practices]. Retrieved from www.ilo.org/wcmsp5/groups/public/-europe/-ro-geneva/-ilo-ankara/documents/publication/wcms_799679.pdf

Kazanoğlu, N. (2019). Work and family life reconciliation policies in Turkey: Europeanisation or Ottomanization? *Social Sciences*, 8(2), 36.

Kocamiş, T. U., & Yildirim, G. (2016). Sustainability reporting in Turkey: Analysis of companies in the BIST sustainability index. *European Journal of Economics and Business Studies*, 2(3), 41–51.

Kolaşin, G. U., Uncu, P. H., Cansuz, Y., & Yasemin, K. (2015). *Türkiye'de lise ve üniversite mezunu kadınların işgücüne katılım kararlarının incelenmesi* [Examining the labor force participation decisions of high school and university graduate women in Turkey]. TÜBİTAK Report, No. 113K365. Ankara. Retrieved from http://betam.bahcesehir.edu.tr/category/ea/

Küskü, F., Aracı, Ö., & Özbilgin, M. F. (2021). What happens to diversity at work in the context of a toxic triangle? Accounting for the gap between discourses and practices of diversity management. *Human Resource Management Journal*, 31(2), 553–574. https://doi.org/10.1111/1748-8583.12324

Lu, J., Ren, L., Zhang, C., Liang, M., Stasiulis, N., & Streimikis, J. (2020). Impacts of feminist ethics and gender on the implementation of CSR initiatives. *Filosofija. Sociologija*, 31(1).

Özbilgin, M., & Slutskaya, N. (2017). Consequences of neo-liberal politics on equality and diversity at work in Britain: Is resistance futile? In Chanlat, J.-F., & Özbligin, M. F. (Eds.), *Management and Diversity* (*International Perspectives on Equality, Diversity and Inclusion*) (Vol. 4, pp. 319–334). Emerald Publishing Limited. https://doi.org/10.1108/S2051-233320160000004015

Özbilgin, M., Tatli, A., Ipek, G., & Sameer, M. (2016). Four approaches to accounting for diversity in global organisations. *Critical Perspectives on Accounting*, 35, 88–99. https://doi.org/10.1016/j.cpa.2015.05.006

Özbilgin, M., & Tatli, A. (2011). Mapping out the field of equality and diversity: Rise of individualism and voluntarism. *Human Relations*, 64(9), 1229–1253. https://doi.org/10.1177/0018726711413620

Özçelik, F., Öztürk, B. A., & Gürsakal, S. (2015). Corporate sustainability: A research on firms that issue sustainability reports in Turkey. *Business and Economics Research Journal*, 6(3), 33.

Ozdora-Aksak, E., & Atakan-Duman, S. (2016). Gaining legitimacy through CSR: An analysis of Turkey's 30 largest corporations. *Business Ethics: A European Review*, 25(3), 238–257.

Özsoy, Z., Şenyücel, M., & Oba, B. (2021). *Gender Diversity in the Top Management Teams of Turkish Listed Companies*. 12th ICMS Conference, BML Munjal University, 16–18 December 2021.

PERYON. (n.d.). *Ödül kategorileri* [Reward Categories]. Retrieved from www.peryon.org.tr/odul-kategorileri

Pitts, D. W., Hicklin, A. K., Hawes, D. P., & Melton, E. (2010). What drives the implementation of diversity management programs? Evidence from public organizations. *Journal of Public Administration Research and Theory*, 20, 867–886. https://doi.org/10.1093/jopart/mup044

Plitmann, Y. (2022). Authentic compliance with a symbolic legal standard? How critical race theory can change institutionalist studies on diversity in the workplace. *Law & Social Inquiry*, 47(1), 331–346. https://doi.org/10.1017/lsi.2021.38

Sun, S. L., Zhu, J., & Ye, K. (2015). Board openness during an economic crisis. *Journal of Business Ethics*, 129(2), 363–377. https://doi.org/10.1007/s10551-014-2164-1

Syed, J., & Özbilgin, M. (2019). *Managing Diversity and Inclusion: An International Perspective*. Sage.

Szydlo, M. (2015). Gender Equality on the Boards of EU Companies: Between Economic Efficiency, Fundamental Rights and Democratic Legitimisation of Economic Governance, *European Law Journal*, 21 (1), 97–115. http://dx.doi.org/10.1111/eulj.12074

Takagi, J., & Gröschl, S. (2012). Introduction: Gender quotas. In Gröschl, S., & Takagi, J. (Eds.), *Diversity Quotas, Diverse Perspectives: The Case of Gender*. Routledge.

Tatli, A. (2011). A multi-layered exploration of the diversity management field: Diversity discourses, practices and practitioners in the UK. *British Journal of Management*, 22(2), 238–253. https://doi.org/10.1111/j.1467-8551.2010.00730.x

TÜİK. (2017) *Aile yapısı araştırması, 2016* [Family Structure Research 2016]. Retrieved from www.tuik.gov.tr/PreHaberBultenleri.do;jsessionid=4l2FZ1kVpNL8JhhkfQtRLqmnJtJ6x 4l2FZ1kVpNL8JhhkfQtRLqmnJtJ6xk6sGXGwbChqTR9N0LY1K1bp!1813643467?id=21869

TÜİK.(2022).*İstatistiklerdekadın2021*[WomeninStatistics2021].Retrievedfromhttps://data.tuik.gov.tr/Bulten/Index?p=Istatistiklerle-Kadin-2021-45635#:~:text=Tper centC3per cent9Cper centC4per centB0Kper cent20Kurumsal&text=Adreseper cent20Dayalper centC4per centB1per cent20Nper centC3per centBCfusper cent-20Kayper centC4per centB1tper cent20Sistemi,1'iniper cent20iseper cent20er-keklerper cent20oluper centC5per cent9Fturdu

Ulutaş, Ç. Ü. (2015). İş ve aile yaşamını uzlaştırma politikaları: Türkiye'de yeni politika arayışları [Policies of reconciling work and family life: Searching for new policies in Turkey]. *Ankara Üniversitesi SBF Dergisi*, 70(3), 723–750. https://doi.org/10.1501/SBFder_0000002368

Yang, Y., & Konrad, A. M. (2011). Understanding diversity management practices: Implications of institutional theory and resource-based theory. *Group & Organization Management*, 36(1), 6–38. https://doi.org/10.1177/1059601110390997

Discussion and conclusion

This book was prompted by a simple observation in relation to gender diversity and inclusion practices of publicly listed companies in Turkey: A disparity between what is publicly announced by these corporations and what is actually done. Although in their CSR and sustainability reports these companies provide information about their sensitivity to gender diversity issues, women in these workplaces still encounter discriminatory practices such as wage inequality for similar jobs, motherhood pay gap, and unequal employment and promotion opportunities. As reported by the WEF Global Gender Gap Report 2021, the presence of women in the upper echelons as members of boards of director is fairly low (18.10 percent) when compared to their male (81.90 percent) counterparts. The situation is even more dire in top management positions; only 3.90 percent of companies employ women as top professional managers.

During our field study, we saw that the majority of these "voluntarily" done CSR activities for gender diversity and inclusion were limited to training projects and aimed for the betterment of human resources so that there would be improvements in the company's creativity, innovation, and service quality performance. In other words, companies do not perceive gender diversity as a human rights issue. Instead, gender diversity and inclusion are instrumentalised to attract consumers and investors and to construct a socially responsible corporate image. Listed companies invest their prestige in diversity and inclusion programs with the expectation that they will acquire a favourable reputation and accompanying economic gains.

Given this background, the next question that guided us as we wrote this book was this: Why is there such a disparity between the talk and walk of publicly listed Turkish companies? At this stage, Bourdieu's concept of the field and the framework developed by Tatli (2011) for a multi-layered analysis of the gender diversity discourse, practices, and practitioners guided us. Besides listed companies, we decided to also study the discourse and practices of other actors – the state, NGOs, international organisations, and

DOI: 10.4324/9781003244868-9

trade unions – that are influential in shaping the Turkish gender diversity field. Such an approach is useful in identifying power positions taken and stakes in being part of the field that is demarcated and thus identifying the peculiarity of the Turkish experience.

In Turkey throughout its history, two salient issues have been extremely influential in shaping the discourse and practices of all the related actors in relation to diversity and inclusion: The persistence of the patriarchal culture and the pivotal role attributed to and assumed by the state in economic and social realms. Due to the patriarchal culture, the traditional gender roles ascribed for women in society are dependency on the male members of the family, caregiving for children and the elderly, and supporting husbands – the main breadwinners of the family – in pursuing their careers. These traditional roles are internalised by women. In most cases, even if they are equipped with the education and capabilities to go out into the workplace, women prefer to stay at home in the service of family members.

The state has always been involved in women's issues to varying degrees, with different ideological emphasis, and in different ways for building alliances with non-state actors. During the early Republican period, the major concern of the state cadres was for women's rights, and women were given the rights to receive an education, enter the labour market, and be represented in politics. In this top-down process, the relationship between the state and the non-state actor (only one organization at that time, the Turkish Women's Union) was described as co-optation. After the 1980s, the numbers of non-state actors advocating for women's issues increased, and the focus on human rights shifted to gender equality. Through a process identified as "contestation and cooperation", state agencies and non-state actors worked for the elimination of discrimination against women. Accordingly, changes in the criminal and civil code were made, and institutions such as the Directorate on the Status and Problems of Women, women's studies centres in various universities, and a women's library and documentation centre (Kadın Eserleri Kütüphanesi ve Bilgi Merkezi Vakfı) were established. Ratification of CEDAW was an important driving force behind these changes and the inclusion of international non-governmental organisations to gender equality issues in Turkey.

However, from the early 2000s on, the impetus to adopt these positive legal and institutional improvements for gender equality in society and the workplace was weakened when two major developments occurred. The new labour law (4857) drafted in 2003 in line with neoliberal policies pursued by the government and the sharp turn towards conservative Islamist values underlying government policies after the 2011 elections were the main forces underpinning this weakening. The labour law legalised instruments of neoliberalism such as flexible work, part-time work, temporary and contract labour, and subcontracting and incorporated provisions such as extended maternal leave and the obligation to provide childcare in the workplace. However, in the long run, these provisions led to a situation where companies started to employ fewer women or they only employed women in part-time or temporary jobs. During the interviews, one HR director explicated this trend:

> Regulations related to maternity leave seem to be favourable for women, but in the long run, these regulations discourage firms from employing women. Employers question these kinds of regulations. Why would they employ female workers when they can employ male employees to avoid the trouble?

Furthermore, in Turkey, law enforcement is weak, and companies develop various means to sidestep regulations. Another HR director explained the attitude adopted by the companies:

> On paper, regulations require nursery services for women employees. Most of the time companies are ready to pay the penalty, which is a small amount. Government officials never control this. You can easily say that I have an agreement with a nursery for my employees in a distant district of the city which is not possible to commute to easily and thus impossible for the employees to take their children to this remote childcare centre. It is impossible to solve the problem by coercion. It is the responsibility of the state to provide convenient nursery services.

In addition to neoliberal policies and the labour law that led to the weakening of gender equality, the discourse of state officials and the new institutions developed in line with this rhetoric changed. The discourse changed from gender equality to gender justice that "acknowledges the feminine qualities of women . . . devalues policies such as equal opportunities and positive discrimination" (Ün, 2019, pp. 6 and 45). The adoption of such a discourse implied a distancing from a globally accepted norm that was advocated by NGOs that opted for women's rights and efforts to replace it with a local norm reflecting an Islamic view. Changes in discourse accompanied changes in previously established institutions as well; for example, the Ministry of Women and Family Affairs was replaced with the Ministry of Family and Social Policies. This institutional change could be seen as a return to the traditional patriarchal values predominant in Turkish culture: The woman's place is with the family, the woman's main responsibility is to ensure the maintenance of the family, the woman's main role is caregiving. These changes in discourse and institutions were accompanied by the emergence of the new conservative women's organisations that state authorities appointed to represent women's interests in international platforms.

During the last decade, as an outcome of increasing emphasis on family policies and family institutions that emphasised conservative notions of gender roles, distancing from global norms of gender equality, and full-blown implementation of neoliberal policies, diversity management and gender diversity have been sidelined. Ergo, decreased women's participation in the labour force, underrepresentation of women in managerial positions, the denial of LGBTI+ rights, and disinterest in issues of ethnicity increased. Gender diversity and inclusion became issues of corporate social responsibility and sustainability that were pursued voluntarily by a few listed companies. One of the antecedents of such corporate activity rested on the prevailing state-business relations in Turkey. The business community expected that the financial risks associated with the implementation of diversity and inclusion programs would be undertaken by the governmental authorities. Also, state actions that were focused on the short-term led to a milieu of uncertainty in which companies preferred to confine their actions to legal constraints and to defer their legal responsibilities with an expectation of future changes.

The driving rationale of the state authorities and listed companies in assuming a pivotal role in implementing and maintaining gender diversity programs can be explained in relation to their attempts to either become self-sustained entities or to maintain state-business relations. They expected to be able to control the rules of the game and, if needed, to subvert the rules for their own needs. For example, TÜSİAD, representing secular big capital, tried to influence government authorities for the establishment of public nurseries, which otherwise would have been the responsibility of their member companies. Similarly, we have seen that, through various lobbying efforts, listed companies opted for the ratification of omnibus laws and legal amendments to legitimise short-term flexible work arrangements that would render women as a part-time, temporary workforce.

Against all expectations, gender diversity is not the central issue in the current agenda of Turkish trade unions, no matter which political wing they subscribe to. Left-wing trade unions focus on the devastating effects of neoliberal policies on de-unionisation, the exclusion of unions from the decision-making process, the weakening of the bargaining power of the employees due to flexible labour, and subcontracting. Both left-wing and pro-Islamist right-wing unions mainstream gender equality (Tabak & Doğan, 2022). Right-wing, pro-Islam unions, in a pro-government attitude, support gender justice and thus women's issues on their agenda are marginalised. Left-wing trade unions, in discourse, adhere to the gender equality norm, but they do not follow the premises of gender equality in their own organisations. There are no women in their management cadres, and women are excluded in the process (Türer, 2020). One exceptional case is DİSK, which is run by a woman president. This being said, we can still claim that trade unions are not in the game at all.

NGOs focusing on women's issues and aiming for the betterment of women in social, political, and economic realms (such as KEIG, KEP, KADAV, and KADER) work on gender equality and diversity. They are dedicated advocates of issues such as the elimination of sexual harassment, inequality in wages, male domination, and worsening working conditions. However, their efforts are limited to the reports prepared and concerns voiced; business circles do not see them as a stakeholder, nor do they aim to be part of the gender diversity initiatives taken by companies. Somehow, there is a breach in the harmonious relationship between them and the corporate actors of the diversity field. We can call their efforts "good intentions" without deliberate outcomes. The responses of these NGOs are more directed towards the actions taken by the government. Especially after 2011 with the emergence of a new group of NGOs who support gender justice and conservative and Islamic values as discussed above (such as KADEM, AK-DER, and KASAD-D), the formerly established women's organisations that opt for gender equality lost their central position in influencing the actions taken by the state in relation to women's issues.

Another group of NGOs, that are mainly established by business circles, are engaged in awareness-raising campaigns for gender equality and inclusion of women in the upper echelons, especially on boards of directors. In this vein, contests are organised, awards are given, and best practices are publicly announced. In other words, the activities of this group of NGOs are limited to gender diversity and inclusion for a well-educated, small group of women. Also, it is highly debatable whether through such practices these NGOs contribute directly or even indirectly to the public relations and image-building efforts of big business.

International organisations have a dominant role in the field of gender diversity. Applications related to gender diversity have entered the agenda of Turkish companies through international organisations. A prime example of this is the equality in the workplace initiative. Diversity entered the country's agenda when Turkey was selected for a pilot project by the WEF along with three other countries with a high gender gap. Initially, the project was overseen and supervised by the minister responsible for the family. A year and a half after the start of the project, the minister was reassigned to another post and the project was left unclaimed. At the same time, the AKP government began to move away from Western countries and international organisations. International organisations such as UN Women and the ILO were already bringing many crucial issues in the field of diversity to the country's agenda. However, these efforts did not yield positive results because they were not supported and followed by the state and, most importantly, they were not supported by the necessary legislation. Projects brought to Turkey by international organisations and carried out jointly with the business world cannot be transformative unless they are supported by the state. Unless the studies carried out under the leadership of international organisations are embraced by the Turkish government, they will be limited to awareness-raising, education, and public relations activities.

The major contribution of the work presented in this book is its emphasis on context in explaining the present-day neglect of gender diversity and inclusion in Turkish workplaces. Current research on Turkey focuses on diversity management and has not fully addressed the political, cultural, or social character of the Turkish context, and it consequently has failed to illuminate the organisational dynamics of workforce gender diversity. There are notable studies (for example, Özbilgin & Yalkın, 2019; Özbilgin & Tatli, 2011; Küskü et al., 2021) that explain the interaction among workplace diversity, institutions, and neoliberal policies. This book follows a similar path but, additionally, includes a stream of studies that focus on the women's movement in Turkey for identifying the social, political, and cultural roots of gender diversity and the inclusion practices of Turkish listed companies. Such an approach was useful in identifying two major tropes – the patriarchal culture and state dominance – peculiar to the Turkish context that shaped gender diversity and inclusion in the workplace. The state always had a pivotal role in shaping the agenda regarding gender diversity and inclusion. While adhering to the norms of patriarchal culture is a prevalent issue in all the periods of Turkish history, the discourse adopted and institutions promoted by the state in relation to women issues varied. Ergo, the interaction among the state, big business, non-governmental organisations, and trade unions took different forms, such as co-optation and collaboration-competition. However, especially after 2011, the drastic change in the discourse adopted by the state authorities (gender justice), development of institutions that prioritised family rather than women, and the state's support of conservative NGOs led to confusion as to the power positions to be taken and sides to be supported. In a way, the polarising strategy of the government has extended to NGOs, trade unions, businesses, and a reconfiguration of power relations between state and non-state actors. While those who supported gender equality and diversity were moved to the margins and assumed an oppositional stance, new emerging actors became influential in filling the voids thus created. At this point, it is worth noting that accentuating the role of patriarchal culture and a dominant state does not undermine the role of neoliberal policies in shaping corporate attentions towards employing women. Neoliberal policies, emphasis on corporate financial performance as the major success factor ,and labour laws that legitimise outsourcing and flexible and temporary work led to a competitive business milieu where investments (such as nurseries and maternity leave) for the betterment of work life for women employees are considered to be unnecessary costs that can be avoided by employing more men or employing women in part-time or temporary jobs. We have seen that the struggle for domination in this competitive business environment is based on recognition, prestige, and reputation as well as long-term productivity expectations. The only concern of the listed companies that are engaged in gender diversity programs is to proclaim the value of the program which they are part of.

References

Küskü, F., Aracı, Ö., & Özbilgin, M. F. (2021). What happens to diversity at work in the context of a toxic triangle? Accounting for the gap between discourses and practices of diversity management. *Human Resource Management Journal*, 31(2), 553–574. https://doi.org/10.1111/1748-8583.12324

Özbilgin, M. F., & Tatli, A. (2011). Mapping out the field of equality and diversity: Rise of individualism and voluntarism. *Human Relations*, 64(9), 1229–1253. https://doi.org/10.1177/0018726711413620

Özbilgin, M. F., & Yalkın, C. (2019). Hegemonic dividend and workforce diversity: The case of "biat" and meritocracy in nation branding in Turkey. *Journal of Management & Organization*, 25(4), 543–553. https://doi.org/10.1017/jmo.2019.39

Tabak, H., & Doğan, M. (2022). Global gender equality norm and trade unions in Turkey: Local contestations, rival validations, and discrepant receptions. *Journal of Political Sciences*, 31(1), 53–72. https://doi.org/10.26650/siyasal.2022.31.947376

Tatli, A. (2011). A multi-layered exploration of the diversity management field: Diversity discourses, practices and practitioners in the UK. *British Journal of Management*, 22(2), 238–253. https://doi.org/10.1111/j.1467-8551.2010.00730.x

Türer, A. (2020). *Türkiye'deki üye sendikalarda kadın temsili ve kadına yönelik faaliyetler haritalama çalışması* [Representation of Women in Member Unions in Turkey and Activities for Mapping]. Retrieved July 10, 2022, from https://dspace.ceid.org.tr/xmlui/handle/1/903

Ün, M. B. (2019). Contesting global gender equality norms: The case of Turkey. *Review of International Studies*, 45(5), 828–847. https://doi.org/10.1017/S026021051900024X

Appendix 1

Theoretical background

From the 1980s on, there has been increasing interest among management and organisation studies scholars in the work of Bourdieu (Sieweke, 2014). As noted by Sieweke (2014), both the number and the comprehensiveness of the citations have increased. Notably, the comprehensive studies researchers (Everett, 2002; Tatli & Özbilgin, 2005; Emirbayer & Johnson, 2008) on Bordieuan sociology have been influential in providing a base for advancing research in organisation studies.

Although the attention to Bourdieu in management and organisation studies has increased, scholars have noted the limited number of research projects that use Bourdieu's notions in relation to diversity management (Özbilgin & Tatli, 2011; Tatli, 2011; Tatli & Özbilgin, 2012; Syed & Özbilgin, 2009; Tatli et al., 2012).

The major concepts of Bordieuan sociology – field, capital, and habitus – are linked relationally. This is useful in linking micro-level processes and macro structures in an analysis. It also suggests that, in a specific field, some resources can be more valuable, and organisations are embedded in power relationships in their struggle for these resources as well as the legitimate right to value resources (Swartz, 2008). Accordingly, this study was mainly influenced by Tatli's study (2011) which also conceptualised the diversity field as a social field that is composed of and constructed by the activities of engaged actors and their discourse.

For a relational approach, besides field and capital, habitus can be studied to resolve the dualism between the macro and micro levels of analysis. Habitus "implies knowledge and recognition of the imminent laws of the field, the stake" (Bourdieu, 2005b, p. 76) and is related to individual agents. Habitus exhibits itself in the form of a mental schemata, underlying principles of judgement, and practice shaped by economic and cultural conditions experienced earlier in the life of an individual and modified later by further interactions. "The relationship between habitus and field is dialectical, the field, as a structured space, tends to structure the habitus, while the habitus tends to structure the perceptions of the field" (Bourdieu, 1988, p. 784).

The incorporation of a practice into a field – like diversity management practices – can change the distribution and the form of capital, which in turn can change the habitus – the identities, mental schemes, appreciations, and perceptions. This perspective implies that fields are the arenas of power struggles and tensions (Emirbayer & Johnson, 2008; Tatli & Özbilgin, 2012; Tatli et al., 2012). It is a dynamic, ongoing process, which enables us to explore the agents and organisations and the activities of multiple actors in the enactment, reproduction, and maintenance of social structure (Kyriakidou & Ozbilgin, 2006; Tatli, 2011). Actors exist as socially constituted agents who have qualities to promulgate practices that shape an organisational field. For Bourdieu, any social formation is a system of semiautonomous, multidimensional, hierarchically organised series of fields, which are created by agents. Each field is a structured space, encompassing its own laws, logic, and relations of force. Fields encompass agents and configurations of relationships between the connections in which agents are positioned. In other words, a specific field is conceived as a space of positions as well as of position-takings (Emirbayer & Johnson, 2008).

The interview data provide evidence about the notion of habitus; the individual actors (the managers), while explaining their engagement in diversity programs within their companies, highlighted the role of their previous experiences. These prior experiences, either in childhood or in other companies, helped them to develop a feeling for the game that enabled them to act without prior calculations; they were ready to perceive and practice diversity programs. They opted for responsibility and perceived that such a position-taking was appropriate and desirable. Based on our interview notes, we can also say that these managers were proud of their achievements and stressed their pioneering role. Such a position-taking served to classify diversity program initiators into a better position both by themselves and by other organisational members.

The structure of a field is also shaped by the binding forces. In other words, structure is temporary, and it is a "state of power relations" or a "state of the distribution of the specific capital" (Bourdieu, 1993, p. 73). Thus, fields are characterised by a continuous struggle for domination. Dominant positions, the "force" of an organisation, depend on the structure and the volume of capital – financial, technological, judicial, organisational, and cultural – possessed as well as the degree of valuation attached to that capital in a given field (Bourdieu, 2005b).

In our study, we captured many of the aspects that Bourdieu conceptualised. In the Turkish gender diversity field, dominant positions are secured by listed companies and regulatory agencies. The preliminary analysis of our data reveals that the struggle for domination is based on recognition, prestige, and reputation as well as productivity expectations in the long run. The listed companies that are engaged in diversity programs are not concerned about giving commercial value to these programs; their major concern is to proclaim the value of the program which they advocate and are part of. They invest their prestige in the diversity programs with an expectation of securing a favourable reputation and its accompanying economic gains. Besides the interviews, the analysis of media coverage during the initiation of the Equality in the Workplace platform provides vast evidence about the instrumentalisation of the initiative for corporate image and reputation maintaining efforts.

Appendix 2
Methodology

Following Tatli's study (2011), based on Bourdieu's notion of field and capital, we explored the emergence of a diversity field in Turkey. We focused on macro- and meso-organisational levels, agents, practices, and discourses. Thus, we tried to provide answers to these questions: Why does gender inequality in the workplace persist without resistance? What are the cultural/social values, discourses, and practices that hinder gender diversity? How do engaged actors (the state, firms, and labour unions), in their struggle to attain legitimacy and power, shape agendas related to gender diversity?

Our analysis relied on a modified version of content analysis, which facilitated our research into the identification of agent positions, position-takings, organisational practices, and discourse (Krippendorf, 2004). We examined two types of material; Fourteen in-depth interviews (with managers of listed companies, representatives of labour unions, and consultants) as well as secondary data. Secondary data, which was found on the internet, included administrative documents (Turkish governmental reports on the women's workforce and Turkish law and codes), international reports concerning gender equality and mainstreaming, annual reports of holding companies, Turkish newspaper articles, reports of non-governmental organisations, and literature on diversity management in businesses. These materials aided the research in capturing background information and monitoring the credibility of the interview data.

The analysis consisted of two parts. Firstly, we implemented weekly sessions of desk research on international reports, Turkish administrative documents, and Turkish academic literature on diversity management to gain detailed information on diversity programs of various countries. This aided us in identifying differences between interpretations and the functioning of these practices and discourse. Then, we collected several annual reports and newspaper articles that contained information on the gender equality principles and diversity practices of Turkish holding companies. We borrowed the tradition of Bourdieu's field approach, taking diversity management as a field where various constituencies position themselves in terms of their discourse and actions, and that approach guided us to identify practices that reproduce the gender gap and the neglect of gender diversity practices. Thus, the study is based on longitudinal research carried out by the authors. The primary data was collected via 14 in-depth interviews. For identifying interviewees, we followed purposeful sampling and approached people (managers and consultants) who occupied a position that exclusively dealt with gender diversity initiatives. Similarly, we selected those listed companies that had a special unit dealing with gender diversity issues.

Code	*Gender*	*Affiliation*	*Role*	*Minutes*	*Pages*
A1	Female	Conglomerate	Sustainability and Stakeholder Relations Manager	34	9
O1	Female	Conglomerate / Non-Profit Org.	Corporate Communications and External Affairs Manager / Social Gender Equality Work Group Member	53	11
B1	Male	Conglomerate	Human Resource Manager	41	9
E1	Female	Conglomerate / Non-Profit Org.	Human Resource Manager / Board Member	49	10
S1 K1 C1	Male Male Male	Holding	Demand Planning Manager /Engineer Human Resource Manager/Engineer Human Resource Expert / Engineer	32	11
Y1	Male	Consultant Agency / International Non-Profit Org. / Non-Profit Org.	CEO / Board Member / Board Member	40	10
M1	Male	International Consultant Agency / Non-Profit Org.	Office Leader / Board Member	30	9
O2	Male	Company / Non-Profit Org.	Human Resource Manager / Member	55	6
A2	Female	Holding	Corporate Communications Manager	92	15

Code	*Gender*	*Affiliation*	*Role*	*Minutes*	*Pages*
E2	Female	Labour Union	Consultant	45	7
N1	Female	Labour Union	Organising Specialist	45	9
M2	Male	Labour Union	Manager	29	5
S2	Female	NGO	Coordinator	76	13
N2	Female	Labour Union	Writer	38	9
Total				**659**	**133**

The interviews aimed to map the drivers, scope, and nature of diversity management practices. During the interviews, as well as responding to some of our comments, respondents were also allowed to reflect on their observations as well as related practices of other institutional actors. Interviews were conducted face to face and lasted between 30 and 80 minutes. The interviews were also transcribed verbatim.

Secondary sources exceeded 140 items that are all digital. These sources consist of diversity and inclusion policies, labour statistics, non-profit organisation reports concerned with women's employment status, news articles, and legal documents.

Source	*Type*	*Total number*	*Total number of pages*
Digital sources (pdf/doc/etc)	Diversity and Inclusion Policy of a Turkish Holding Company	5	**9**
	Diversity and Inclusion Policy of an International Company	1	**2**
	Diversity and Inclusion Guide of an International Organisation	2	**75**
	Turkish Government Agency or State Commission Report on Women's Employment	2	**404**
	International Conventions and Agreements	2	**74**
	Turkish Law about Labour/Equality/ Diversity or any other related topic	4	**563**
	Turkish Union Magazine Issue about Women's Employment	1	**29**

(*Continued*)

(Continued)

Source	*Type*	*Total number*	*Total number of pages*
	Turkish Union Magazine Issue about Employment and /or Unemployment	1	**13**
	Turkish Human Resource Association Magazine Issue about Equality	1	56
	Turkish NGO Report about Women's Labour and Employment	10	**511**
	Workshop Notes of a Turkish Association on Diversity and Inclusion	1	**2**
	Political Note of a Turkish University about Diversity	1	**4**
	Turkish University Report about Social Gender Equality	1	**46**
	Diversity and Inclusion Policy of a Turkish University	2	**5**
	Covid-19 and Work Relations Research of a Turkish NGO	1	**37**
	Gender Gap Report of an International Organisation	2	**776**
	Gender Equality report of an International Organisation	2	**104**
	Gender Diversity Index of an International Organisation	1	**100**
	Gender Diversity Report of an International Organisation	1	**24**
	Board Diversity Research of an International Organisation	1	12
	Action Plan of an International Organisation	1	26

Source	*Type*	*Total number*	*Total number of pages*
Web sites of the organisations	Diversity and Inclusion Statements of an International Company	3	**3**
	Diversity and Inclusion Statements of a Turkish Holding Company	3	**3**
	Labour Statistics of Turkey	3	**3**
	Information on Panels/Workshop of a Turkish non-profit org./NGO	2	**2**
	Information on Part Time/Flexible Work Regulations	3	**3**
	Regulation on Turkish Private Nursery and Day Care Services	1	**1**
Newspapers	Information about Workplace Diversity/ Inclusion and Equality	13	**13**
	Information about Women's Employment	11	**11**
	News about Authoritative Politics and Bans	6	**6**
Total		86	**2917**

For the analysis of transcriptions, QDAMiner software was used. Having started the analysis within a deductive approach, we achieved the first insights into Turkish diversity practices by relating these findings to the works of Tatli (2011) and several other studies on Bourdiean sociology. Accordingly, we grouped our findings on actor, purpose, discourse, practice, and triggering event categories, respectively.

Index

Note: Page numbers in **bold** indicate a table and page numbers followed by an n indicate a note on the corresponding page.